TO

_____

FROM

_____

If you like sports and are a follower of Jesus, you may wor
are any people in the sports world who value faith as muc
Actually there are hundreds of them, and their viewpoi
their walk with God can encourage and challenge

Discovery House Publishers is affiliated with RBC Ministries, Grand Rapids, Michigan.

Requests for permission to quote from this calendar should be directed to: Permissions Department, Discovery House Publishers, P.O. Box 3566, Grand Rapids, MI 49501, or contact us by e-mail at permissionsdept@dhp.org

Compiled by Dave Branon
Design by Kris Nelson/StoryLook Design
Cover photo: Superstock/Tetra Images
Interior photos: Thinkstock/Getty Images and Shutterstock

ISBN 978-1-62707-075-1

Printed in China

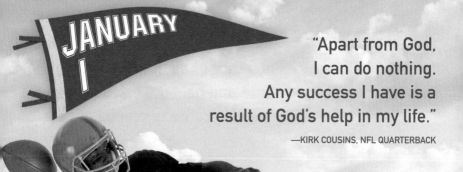

JANUARY
1

"Apart from God,
I can do nothing.
Any success I have is a
result of God's help in my life."

—KIRK COUSINS, NFL QUARTERBACK

Jesus: "I am the vine; you are the branches.
If you remain in me and I in you, you will bear
much fruit; apart from me you can do nothing."

—JOHN 15:5

As a high school quarterback at Holland Christian High School in Michigan,
Kirk Cousins set 35 school records for passing and total offense.

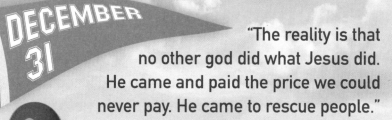

DECEMBER 31

"The reality is that no other god did what Jesus did. He came and paid the price we could never pay. He came to rescue people."

—CLINT GRESHAM, NFL LONG SNAPPER

"This is love: not that we loved God, but that he loved us and sent his Son as an atoning sacrifice for our sins."

—1 JOHN 4:10

Clint Gresham has served as a Young Life leader on Mercer Island in the Seattle area.

JANUARY 2

"I had over 8,000 assists in the NBA, but the greatest pass I ever made was when I gave it all to Jesus Christ."

—MARK JACKSON, NBA ALL-STAR GUARD AND HEAD COACH

"Therefore, if anyone is in Christ, the new creation has come: The old has gone, the new is here!"

—2 CORINTHIANS 5:17

During his NBA career (1987–2004), Mark Jackson scored 12,489 points and handed out 10,334 assists.

DECEMBER 30

"A Christian can rise above any situation to thank God for causing all things to work together for good."

—CASEY SHAW, PRO BASKETBALL PLAYER

"Thanks be to God! He gives us the victory through our Lord Jesus Christ."

—1 CORINTHIANS 15:57

Casey's father-in-law is Homer Drew, longtime men's basketball coach at Valparaiso University.

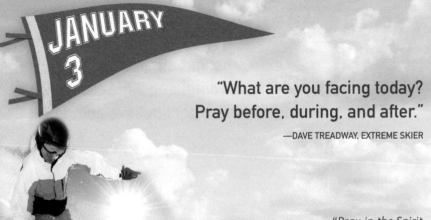

JANUARY
3

"What are you facing today?
Pray before, during, and after."

—DAVE TREADWAY, EXTREME SKIER

"Pray in the Spirit
on all occasions."

—EPHESIANS 6:18

Canadian Dave Treadway is always looking for new adventures. His website says,
"It's normal to spend seven days just getting to a place and skiing for 10 minutes."

DECEMBER 29

"My faith in God is not circumstantial. What I do [snowboarding] and where I am don't determine what I believe about God."

—KELLY CLARK,
US OLYMPIC GOLD MEDAL–WINNING SNOWBOARDER

"For in the gospel the righteousness of God is revealed—a righteousness that is by faith from first to last, just as it is written: 'The righteous will live by faith.' "

—ROMANS 1:17

In addition to her Olympic gold and two bronze in the halfpipe, Kelly Clark has also won X Games superpipe gold medals several times.

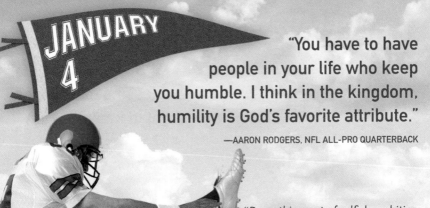

JANUARY 4

"You have to have people in your life who keep you humble. I think in the kingdom, humility is God's favorite attribute."

—AARON RODGERS, NFL ALL-PRO QUARTERBACK

"Do nothing out of selfish ambition or vain conceit. Rather, in humility value others above yourselves."

—PHILIPPIANS 2:3

Aaron Rodgers had to wait for three seasons for Brett Favre to retire before he could become the starting quarterback for the Green Bay Packers.

DECEMBER 28

"God truly delights in blessing us, even as we delight in knowing Him."

—SHANE DOAN, NHL ALL-STAR RIGHT WING

"Blessed rather are those who hear the word of God and obey it."

—LUKE 11:28

Shane Doan started his NHL career with the Winnipeg Jets in 1995, and in 2014 he was still playing for that same franchise, which became the Phoenix Coyotes in 1996.

JANUARY
5

"When I took God into my heart, it was the first true happiness I ever had."

—PETE MARAVICH, NBA HALL OF FAME GUARD

"What do you benefit if you gain the whole world but lose your own soul?"

—MATTHEW 16:26 (NEW LIVING TRANSLATION)

Pete Maravich (1947–1988) was the greatest scorer in college basketball history. He averaged 44 points a game at Louisiana State University in three seasons (3,667 points in 83 games).

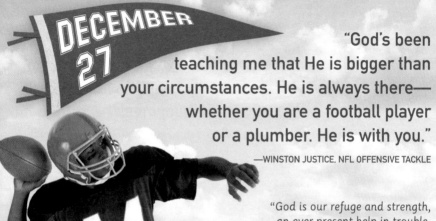

DECEMBER 27

"God's been teaching me that He is bigger than your circumstances. He is always there— whether you are a football player or a plumber. He is with you."

—WINSTON JUSTICE, NFL OFFENSIVE TACKLE

"God is our refuge and strength, an ever-present help in trouble. Therefore we will not fear."

—PSALM 46:1–2

Winston Justice was a second-round pick by the Philadelphia Eagles in 2006. He has played offensive tackle for the Eagles, the Colts, and the Broncos.

JANUARY
6

"I thank God for my trials, because the trials in my life made me a more mature and godly man."

—AVERY JOHNSON, NBA GUARD AND HEAD COACH

"Blessed is the one who perseveres under trials because, having stood the test, that person will receive the crown of life that the Lord has promised to those who love him."

—JAMES 1:12

Avery Johnson played from 1988 through 2004 for six NBA teams, scoring 8,817 points and dishing out 5,846 assists.

DECEMBER 26

"Read the Scriptures.
Stay in it, because sooner or later,
God is going to change you."

—REGGIE WHITE, NFL HALL OF FAME DEFENSIVE LINEMAN

"Sanctify them by the
truth; your word is truth."

—JOHN 17:17

Reggie White (1961–2004) was one of the most celebrated defensive ends in NFL history. He was a 13-time Pro Bowl selection and twice he was the NFL's Defensive Player of the Year. He and his Green Bay Packers teammates won Super Bowl XXXI in 1997.

"Throwing an interception does not change where I stand with God—it's how I deal with the interception that counts."

—TRENT DILFER, NFL QUARTERBACK AND ESPN ANALYST

"We are hard pressed on every side, but not crushed; perplexed, but not in despair."

—2 CORINTHIANS 4:8–9

Trent Dilfer led the Baltimore Ravens to a Super Bowl title in 2001 as the Ravens beat the New York Giants 34–7.

DECEMBER 25

"Whether I win, lose, or draw in sports, Jesus is going to be with me the rest of my life, and I get to spend eternity with Him."

—ELANA MEYERS, OLYMPIC MEDAL–WINNING BOBSLEDDER

"When Christ, who is your life, appears, then you also will appear with him in glory."

—COLOSSIANS 3:4

Elana Meyers won bronze (2010) and silver (2014) medals at the Winter Olympics in the two-woman bobsled. She has also won gold medals at the world championships.

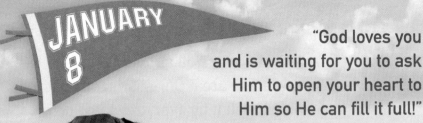

JANUARY 8

"God loves you and is waiting for you to ask Him to open your heart to Him so He can fill it full!"

—SHANNON DUNN-DOWNING, OLYMPIC SNOWBOARDER

"Knock and the door will be opened to you."

—MATTHEW 7:7

Shannon Dunn-Downing won a bronze medal in the halfpipe in the 1998 Winter Olympics in Nagano. She was the first American woman to win an Olympics snowboarding medal.

"You shouldn't have to tell people you are a Christian. They should be able to tell it by everything you do on a daily basis. That's what I strive to do."

—LOVIE SMITH, NFL HEAD COACH

"This, then, is how you ought to regard us: as servants of Christ and as those entrusted with the mysteries God has revealed. Now it is required that those who have been given a trust must prove faithful."

—1 CORINTHIANS 4:1–2

Lovie Smith never played in the NFL. He played college football at the University of Tulsa. His first coaching job was in high school in his hometown of Big Sandy, Texas.

JANUARY
9

"When it seems that God is asking you to wait for something, hold on. He knows what He is doing."

—SHANE DOAN, NHL ALL-STAR RIGHT WING

"Take delight in the LORD, and he will give you the desires of your heart."

—PSALM 37:4

Shane Doan, who grew up in Canada, has competed five times for the Canadian national team in the World Championships of hockey.

"Staying true to my faith in this league is tricky, but it helps knowing I can always count on God for support."

—WES WELKER, NFL ALL-PRO WIDE RECEIVER

"Blessed are those whose ways are blameless, who walk according to the law of the Lord."

—PSALM 119:1

Wes Welker started the Wes Welker Foundation in 2009 to help at-risk kids reach their potential through athletics.

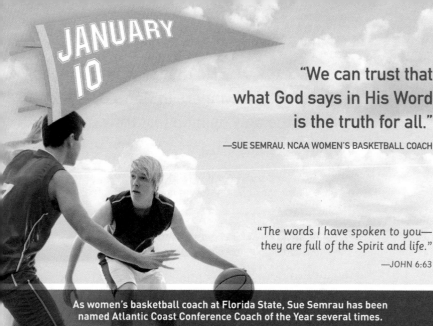

JANUARY 10

"We can trust that what God says in His Word is the truth for all."

—SUE SEMRAU, NCAA WOMEN'S BASKETBALL COACH

"The words I have spoken to you—
they are full of the Spirit and life."

—JOHN 6:63

As women's basketball coach at Florida State, Sue Semrau has been named Atlantic Coast Conference Coach of the Year several times.

"No matter what happens, we can be winners in God's eyes—and His is the only opinion that truly matters."

—JON KITNA, NFL QUARTERBACK

"Whatever you do, work at it with all your heart, as working for the Lord, not for human masters."

—COLOSSIANS 3:23

"For he chose us in him before the creation of the world to be holy and blameless in his sight."

—EPHESIANS 1:4

In late 2013, Jon Kitna signed a one-week contract to back up Kyle Orton for the Dallas Cowboys—and donated his salary to the school where he taught math at the time.

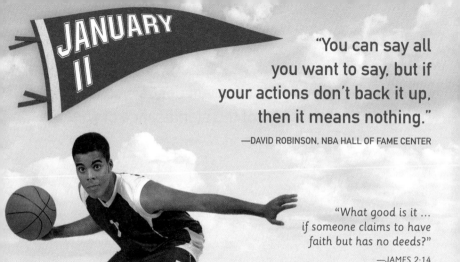

JANUARY 11

"You can say all you want to say, but if your actions don't back it up, then it means nothing."

—DAVID ROBINSON, NBA HALL OF FAME CENTER

"What good is it ... if someone claims to have faith but has no deeds?"

—JAMES 2:14

In the NBA David Robinson won a scoring title, was named to the All-Star team 10 times, and won two championships.

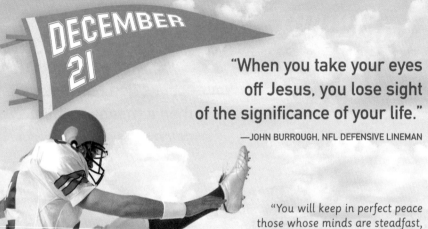

DECEMBER
21

"When you take your eyes
off Jesus, you lose sight
of the significance of your life."

—JOHN BURROUGH, NFL DEFENSIVE LINEMAN

"You will keep in perfect peace
those whose minds are steadfast,
because they trust in you."

—ISAIAH 26:3

While in college, former NFL defensive end
John Burrough studied physics and geophysics.

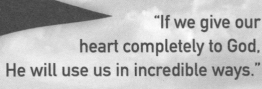

JANUARY 12

"If we give our heart completely to God, He will use us in incredible ways."

—RYAN HALL, OLYMPIC LONG-DISTANCE RUNNER

"[They] will be instruments for special purposes, made holy."

—2 TIMOTHY 2:21

Ryan Hall was on the US Olympic team in 2008 and 2012.

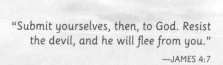

DECEMBER 20

"It is important to be on Jesus' team—for no single person can defeat the devil alone."

—DAVID THOMPSON, NBA HALL OF FAME FORWARD

"Submit yourselves, then, to God. Resist the devil, and he will flee from you."

—JAMES 4:7

You can read about David Thompson's struggles and triumphs in his book *Skywalker*.

"If we follow God's plan in the Word, we'll begin to understand what God wants us to do as we train to be leaders for Him."

—CHARLIE WARD, HEISMAN TROPHY WINNER, NBA GUARD

"Train yourself to be godly."

—1 TIMOTHY 4:7

Charlie Ward was drafted by the New York Knicks in 1994, and he played 11 seasons in the NBA.

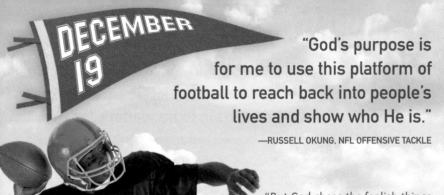

DECEMBER 19

"God's purpose is for me to use this platform of football to reach back into people's lives and show who He is."

—RUSSELL OKUNG, NFL OFFENSIVE TACKLE

"But God chose the foolish things of the world to shame the wise; God chose the weak things of the world to shame the strong."

—1 CORINTHIANS 1:27

Russell Okung was selected to play in the 2012 Pro Bowl. In 2014 he played in the Super Bowl as the Seattle Seahawks beat Denver.

JANUARY 14

"God has been teaching me to stay humble. I never try to get too high or too low. As quickly as success comes, it can be taken away."

—PEYTON SIVA, NBA GUARD

"Humble yourselves, therefore, under God's mighty hand, that he may lift you up in due time."

—1 PETER 5:6

Peyton Siva helped lead Louisville to the NCAA Men's national championship in 2013. He was an Academic All-American at Louisville.

"I think it's a real process of trust and trusting in the Lord that He is in complete control. My faith has always been a very simple faith and in just knowing that God is in control of all the situations and we just trust in Him with all that we have."

—MIKE GARTNER, NHL HALL OF FAME RIGHT WING

"And we know that in all things God works for the good of those who love him, who have been called according to his purpose."

—ROMANS 8:28

During Mike Gartner's distinguished NHL career (1979–1998), he played in 1,432 games and scored 1,335 points, putting him 30th on the all-time pro hockey list.

JANUARY 15

"If I mess up, and I do,
I know that God knows my heart.
I can count on Him to help
me through it."

—LUKE RIDNOUR, NBA GUARD

"Let us then approach God's throne of grace
with confidence, so that we may receive mercy
and find grace to help us in our time of need."

—HEBREWS 4:16

In seven of Luke Ridnour's first ten years in the NBA,
he averaged at least ten points a game.

DECEMBER 17

"There are all kinds of stumbling blocks at this level, but I've surrounded myself with guys who are grounded in Christ."

—JORDY NELSON, NFL WIDE RECEIVER

"As iron sharpens iron, so one person sharpens another."

—PROVERBS 27:17

After playing college ball at Kansas State, Jordy Nelson was drafted by the Green Bay Packers in 2008. In 2011 Nelson caught 68 passes for 1,263 yards.

JANUARY 16

"I understand this is a platform God has given me. I just have to make sure I conduct myself in a way that pleases Him."

—JEREMY LIN, NBA GUARD

"Am I now trying to win the approval of human beings, or of God? Or am I trying to please people? If I were still trying to please people, I would not be a servant of Christ."

—GALATIANS 1:10

After playing at Harvard, Jeremy Lin joined the NBA in 2010. In 2012 he averaged 14 points a game for the New York Knicks.

DECEMBER 16

"Christianity is not a religion, but a person: Jesus Christ and a relationship with Him. Through Him, we have eternal life, for this life is so temporary."

—PETE MARAVICH, NBA HALL OF FAME GUARD

"If you declare with your mouth, 'Jesus is Lord,' and believe in your heart that God raised him from the dead, you will be saved."

—ROMANS 10:9

Pete Maravich was named to the 50 Greatest NBA Players list in 1996 when the league celebrated its 50th anniversary. Maravich led the league in scoring in 1976–1977 with a 31.1 points per game mark.

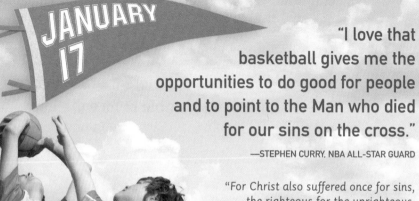

JANUARY 17

"I love that basketball gives me the opportunities to do good for people and to point to the Man who died for our sins on the cross."

—STEPHEN CURRY, NBA ALL-STAR GUARD

"For Christ also suffered once for sins, the righteous for the unrighteous, to bring you to God. He was put to death in the body but made alive in the Spirit."

—1 PETER 3:18

The Golden State Warriors drafted Stephen Curry in 2009, and he averaged 19 points a game in his first three years. In February 2013 he scored 54 points in a game against the Knicks.

"God wants us to focus
on Him. Before there is honor,
I have to be humble before the Lord."

—JON KITNA, NFL QUARTERBACK

"Humble yourselves before the
Lord, and he will lift you up."

—JAMES 4:10

After his NFL career ended in 2011, Jon Kitna returned to his alma mater,
Lincoln High School in Tacoma, Washington, to teach math and coach football.

JANUARY 18

"Our ultimate goal is to be pleasing to the Lord; we should do any and everything to accomplish that goal."

—DAVID THOMPSON, NBA HALL OF FAME FORWARD

"In the same way, faith by itself, if it is not accompanied by action, is dead."

—JAMES 2:17

Known as "Skywalker" because of his incredible vertical leaping ability as a star for North Carolina State, David Thompson led the Wolfpack to the NCAA title in 1974.

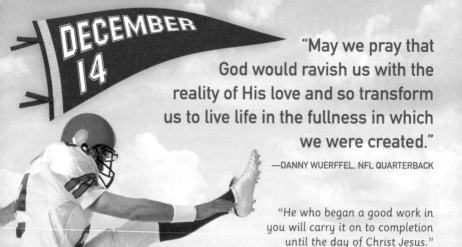

DECEMBER 14

"May we pray that God would ravish us with the reality of His love and so transform us to live life in the fullness in which we were created."

—DANNY WUERFFEL, NFL QUARTERBACK

"He who began a good work in you will carry it on to completion until the day of Christ Jesus."

—PHILIPPIANS 1:6

During his career at Florida, Danny Wuerffel completed 708 of 1,170 passes for 10,875 yards, 114 touchdowns, and one Heisman Trophy.

JANUARY 19

"I play football to glorify Jesus Christ. He came to set me free and give me joy."

—CLINT GRESHAM, NFL LONG SNAPPER

"With one mind and one voice ... glorify the God and Father of our Lord Jesus Christ."

—ROMANS 15:6

Clint Gresham was a member of the Seattle Seahawks, who won Super Bowl XLVIII in New Jersey on February 2, 2014.

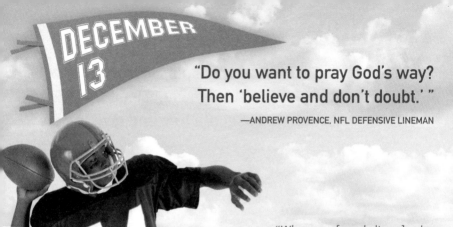

DECEMBER 13

"Do you want to pray God's way?
Then 'believe and don't doubt.'"

—ANDREW PROVENCE, NFL DEFENSIVE LINEMAN

"When you [as a believer] asks,
you must believe and not doubt."

—JAMES 1:6

Andrew Provence and his wife, Angie, have nine children. He works with Athletes in Action. She helps direct the drama ministry at their church in Fayetteville, Georgia.

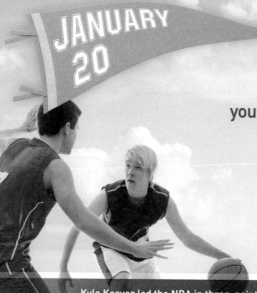

JANUARY 20

"When you're trying to live for Jesus, you're much more stable."

—KYLE KORVER, NBA GUARD

"Whoever walks in integrity walks securely, but whoever takes crooked paths will be found out."

—PROVERBS 10:9

Kyle Korver led the NBA in three-point field goal percentage in 2009–2010 by hitting 59 of 110 shots beyond the arc (.536 percent).

DECEMBER 12

"Are you training to be a tough Christian? Don't slack off. The hard work will be worth it!"

—CHARLIE WARD, NBA GUARD

"The hardworking farmer should be the first to receive a share of the crops."

—2 TIMOTHY 2:6

After his NBA career, Charlie Ward became football coach at Westbury Christian High School in Houston, Texas. In 2014 he moved to Pensacola, Florida, to become head football coach at Booker T. Washington High School.

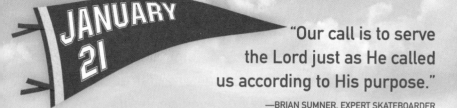

JANUARY 21

"Our call is to serve the Lord just as He called us according to His purpose."

—BRIAN SUMNER, EXPERT SKATEBOARDER

"He has saved us and called us to a holy life—not because of anything we have done but because of his own purpose and grace."

—2 TIMOTHY 1:9

Brian Sumner was a stunt double in the 2003 movie *Grind*, doing skating tricks for Adam Brody.

"If television, the Internet, and other things are distracting us, we need to 'fix our eyes on Jesus.' We must keep our eyes on the target."

—KEN MOYER, NFL OFFENSIVE LINEMAN

"Join with me in suffering, like a good soldier of Christ Jesus."

—2 TIMOTHY 2:3

After his career in the NFL ended, Ken Moyer became a math teacher in Cincinnati. He also has served as the Bengals' team chaplain through Athletes in Action.

"There's nothing that goes on where God goes 'Oops, I missed that one.' Every circumstance that happens in life, God has control of."

—MATT WARE, FORMER HIGH SCHOOL ATHLETE

" 'For my thoughts are not your thoughts, neither are your ways my ways,' declares the Lord. 'As the heavens are higher than the earth, so are my ways higher than your ways and my thoughts than your thoughts.' "

—ISAIAH 55:8–9

Matt Ware was a high school basketball player in Indiana in 1998 when he was injured in practice, suffering permanent paralysis.

DECEMBER 10

"You have to use your talents and abilities to glorify God."

—PEYTON SIVA, NBA GUARD

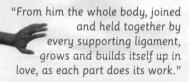

"From him the whole body, joined and held together by every supporting ligament, grows and builds itself up in love, as each part does its work."

—EPHESIANS 4:16

After his college career at Louisville, Peyton Siva was drafted by the Detroit Pistons in the 2013 NBA draft. A few weeks later, he married his college sweetheart, Patience McCroskey.

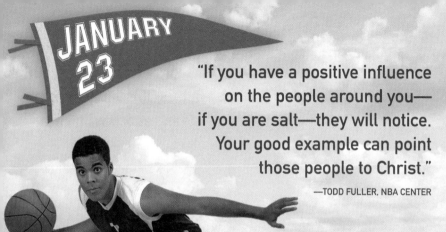

JANUARY 23

"If you have a positive influence on the people around you—if you are salt—they will notice. Your good example can point those people to Christ."

—TODD FULLER, NBA CENTER

"You are the salt of the earth."

—MATTHEW 5:13

After a successful career at North Carolina State, Todd Fuller spent five years in the NBA with Golden State, Utah, Charlotte, and Miami.

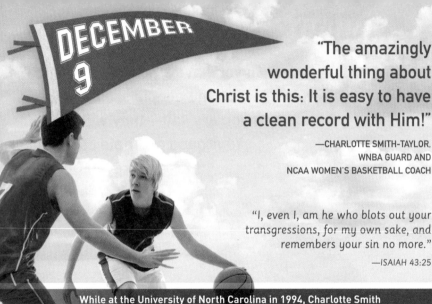

DECEMBER 9

"The amazingly wonderful thing about Christ is this: It is easy to have a clean record with Him!"

—CHARLOTTE SMITH-TAYLOR,
WNBA GUARD AND
NCAA WOMEN'S BASKETBALL COACH

"I, even I, am he who blots out your transgressions, for my own sake, and remembers your sin no more."

—ISAIAH 43:25

While at the University of North Carolina in 1994, Charlotte Smith won the NCAA championship game with a buzzer-beating three-pointer as the Tar Heels beat Louisiana Tech 60–59.

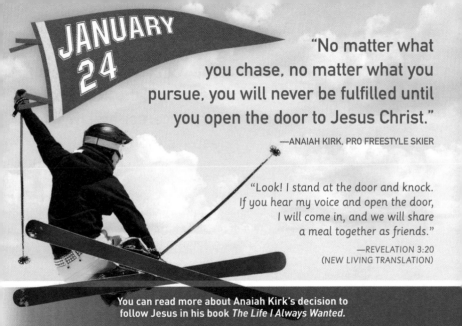

JANUARY 24

"No matter what you chase, no matter what you pursue, you will never be fulfilled until you open the door to Jesus Christ."

—ANAIAH KIRK, PRO FREESTYLE SKIER

"Look! I stand at the door and knock. If you hear my voice and open the door, I will come in, and we will share a meal together as friends."

—REVELATION 3:20
(NEW LIVING TRANSLATION)

You can read more about Anaiah Kirk's decision to follow Jesus in his book *The Life I Always Wanted.*

"Jesus is really in charge. He says, 'You don't take the reins, I do.' He's really in charge of my career and my life. Jesus is there for you too."

—MIKE FISHER, NHL CENTER

"Does not the potter have the right to make out of the same lump of clay some pottery for special purposes and some for common use?"

—ROMANS 9:21

During the offseason, Mike Fisher often works with Hockey Ministries International participating in hockey camps for kids.

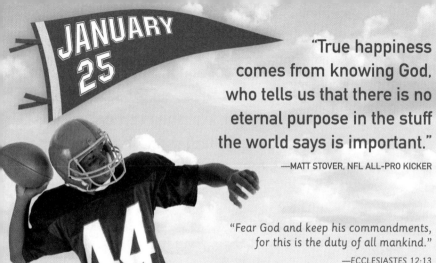

JANUARY 25

"True happiness comes from knowing God, who tells us that there is no eternal purpose in the stuff the world says is important."

—MATT STOVER, NFL ALL-PRO KICKER

"Fear God and keep his commandments, for this is the duty of all mankind."

—ECCLESIASTES 12:13

In his career Matt Stover scored 2,004 points, which at the time of his retirement made him fifth all-time in scoring in NFL history.

"Our responsibility as Christians is to keep our eyes on the Lord, to stay focused on Him. We must remember this: 'I can do everything through [Jesus] who gives me strength' (Philippians 4:13)."

—JAKE VOSKUHL, NBA FORWARD

"I can do all this through [Jesus] who gives me strength."
—PHILIPPIANS 4:13

Jake Voskuhl was drafted by the Chicago Bulls in the 2000 NBA draft. He spent his NBA career playing for the Bulls, the Suns, the Bobcats, the Bucks, and the Raptors.

JANUARY 26

"The peace I get from God is what carried me through [an injury]. I know if I'd had to just rely on my emotions and what I know, my recovery wouldn't have happened."

—NATE ADAMS, MOTOCROSS RIDER

"Let the peace of Christ rule in your hearts."

—COLOSSIANS 3:15

Nate Adams won a gold medal at the 2004 X Games.

DECEMBER 6

"When the devil gets the best of you, you have to come back the next day harder and stronger."

—CHRIS KAMAN, NBA ALL-STAR CENTER

"Your enemy the devil prowls around like a roaring lion looking for someone to devour. Resist him, standing firm in the faith."

—1 PETER 5:8–9

After playing basketball for tiny Tri-Unity Christian High School in Grand Rapids, Michigan, Kaman attended Central Michigan University. There he developed into a first-round NBA draft pick in 2003. He has played for the LA Clippers, New Orleans, Dallas, and the LA Lakers.

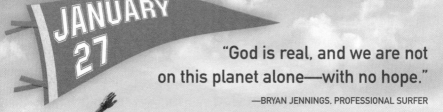

JANUARY 27

"God is real, and we are not on this planet alone—with no hope."

—BRYAN JENNINGS, PROFESSIONAL SURFER

"Hear my cry, O God; listen to my prayer. From the ends of the earth I call to you."

—PSALM 61:1–2

Bryan Jennings became a professional surfer at the age of 18. Later he founded Walking on Water, a Christian surf ministry.

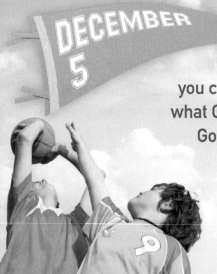

DECEMBER
5

"If you read the Bible, you can have an understanding of what God wants you to do and how God wants you to live your life."

—DARRELL ARMSTRONG, NBA GUARD AND COACH

"Do your best to present yourself to God as one approved, a worker who does not need to be ashamed and who correctly handles the word of truth."

—2 TIMOTHY 2:15

After spending 13 years in the NBA as a player, Darrell Armstrong became an assistant coach for the Dallas Mavericks.

JANUARY 28

"Want to know what to do?
Give God the situation in prayer,
and then trust the guidance of our great
Counselor, the Holy Spirit."

—TODD FULLER, NBA CENTER

"I will ask the Father, and he will give
you another advocate [the Holy Spirit]."

—JOHN 14:16

During his NBA career, Todd Fuller scored 835 points and pulled down 674 rebounds.

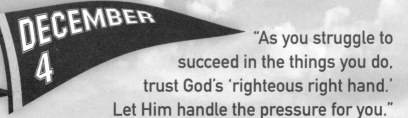

DECEMBER 4

"As you struggle to succeed in the things you do, trust God's 'righteous right hand.' Let Him handle the pressure for you."

—DEB PATTERSON, NCAA WOMEN'S BASKETBALL COACH

"I will uphold you with my righteous right hand."

—ISAIAH 41:10

Deb Patterson was named Big 12 Coach of the Year for her efforts with the Kansas State Wildcats in 2002 and 2008.

"We need to daily remind ourselves who we live for and what our ultimate goal is in life."

—LEIGHANN DOAN REIMER, CANADIAN BASKETBALL STAR

"We make it our goal to please him, whether we are at home in the body or away from it."

—2 CORINTHIANS 5:9

Leighann Doan received the Howard Mackie Award as the best female athlete in a Canadian university in 2001. Her brother is Shane Doan of the NHL.

"My rock is God. I know that if everything were to fall away tomorrow—my family, my wealth, my finances, my racing—I would still have God. And that's the most important."

—GREG ALBERTYN, MOTOCROSS CHAMPION

"The Lord is my rock, my fortress and my deliverer; my God is my rock, in whom I take refuge, my shield and the horn of my salvation, my stronghold."

—PSALM 18:2

In 1999 Greg Albertyn won the American Motorcyclist Association National Championships aboard a Suzuki. He retired in 2000, but he continues to ride in some motocross events.

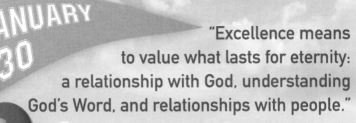

JANUARY 30

"Excellence means
to value what lasts for eternity:
a relationship with God, understanding
God's Word, and relationships with people."

—FRANK REICH, NFL QUARTERBACK AND COACH

"I write these things to you who
believe in the name of the Son of God so
that you may know that you have eternal life."

—1 JOHN 5:13

Frank Reich was an NFL quarterback for 13 seasons with
Buffalo, Carolina, the New York Jets, and Detroit.

DECEMBER 2

"I'd like to thank my Lord and Savior Jesus Christ for this win."

—DEREK ERNST
UPON WINNING HIS FIRST
PGA TOURNAMENT IN 2013

"Give thanks in all circumstances; for this is God's will for you in Christ Jesus."

—1 THESSALONIANS 5:18

Derek Ernst, who played college golf at UNLV, won the Wells Fargo Championship on the PGA Tour in May 2013 when he was just shy of his 23rd birthday.

JANUARY 31

"My faith is a comfort, and it gives me a different reason to be doing my sport."

—CATRIONA LEMAY DOAN,
OLYMPIC GOLD MEDAL–WINNING SPEED SKATER

"The Lord is my light and
my salvation—whom shall I fear?
The Lord is the stronghold of my life."

—PSALM 27:1

Catriona LeMay Doan captured two Olympic gold medals during her speed skating career for Canada. She won the 500-meter race in 1998 and in 2002.

DECEMBER 1

"Jesus alone can fill the emptiness we all have in our lives."

—MATT STOVER, NFL ALL-PRO KICKER

"Grasp how wide and long and high and deep is the love of Christ, and ... know this love that surpasses knowledge."

—EPHESIANS 3:18–19

After he retired from the NFL, Matt Stover began training kickers using something called Spark Motion—an app that enables him to analyze videos uploaded by young kickers.

FEBRUARY 1

"Nobody can stop
what God has for you."

—RUSSELL WILSON, NFL QUARTERBACK

"Trust in the Lord with all your heart
and lean not on your own understanding;
in all your ways submit to him, and
he will make your paths straight."

—PROVERBS 3:5–6

In his second year in the NFL, Russell Wilson led the Seattle Seahawks
to their first championship in Super Bowl XLVIII.

NOVEMBER 30

"Through my relationship with God I learned who I was, and was comfortable in who I was."

—KELLY CLARK,
US OLYMPIC GOLD MEDAL–WINNING SNOWBOARDER

"See what great love the Father has lavished on us, that we should be called children of God! And that is what we are!"

—1 JOHN 3:1

Kelly Clark won a gold medal in snowboarding halfpipe in the 2002 Winter Olympics in Salt Lake City, and she captured bronze in the 2010 Games in Vancouver and the 2014 Games in Sochi, Russia.

FEBRUARY
2

"God is looking for young people who are fully committed to Him."

—JON KITNA, NFL QUARTERBACK

"Love the Lord your God with all your heart and with all your soul and with all your mind."

—MATTHEW 22:37

Jon Kitna began his NFL career in 1996 with the Seattle Seahawks, and he played in the league from 1996 until 2011.

NOVEMBER 29

"There are a lot more blessings in a 'God plan' than in a 'me plan.' "

—ANNE SCHLEPER, US OLYMPIC HOCKEY DEFENSEMAN

"He made known to us the mystery of his will according to his good pleasure."

—EPHESIANS 1:9

While playing for the Minnesota Golden Gophers hockey team in 2011, Anne Schleper was awarded the Big Ten Outstanding Sportsmanship Award.

FEBRUARY 3

"Godliness.
That's what we must value most."

—KYLE BRADY, NFL TIGHT END

"Among you there must not be
even a hint of sexual immorality."

—EPHESIANS 5:3

Kyle Brady was drafted by the NY Jets in the 1995 NFL draft. For the next 13 seasons, he played tight end for the Jets, the Jacksonville Jaguars, and the New England Patriots.

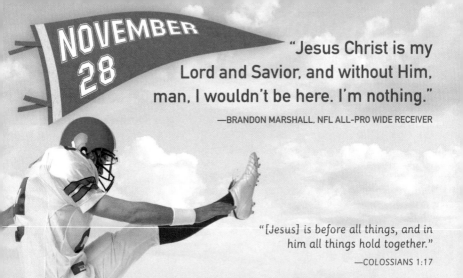

NOVEMBER 28

"Jesus Christ is my Lord and Savior, and without Him, man, I wouldn't be here. I'm nothing."

—BRANDON MARSHALL, NFL ALL-PRO WIDE RECEIVER

"[Jesus] is before all things, and in him all things hold together."

—COLOSSIANS 1:17

In 2009, Brandon Marshall set an NFL record by catching 21 passes in one game while with the Denver Broncos.

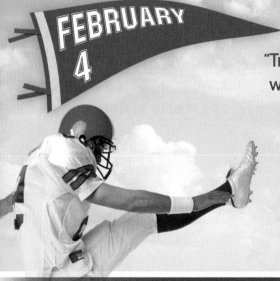

FEBRUARY 4

"Try to be like Christ—
walk consistently and
mirror His image."

—BEN UTECHT, NFL TIGHT END

"Whoever claims to live in
him must live as Jesus did."

—1 JOHN 2:6

Ben Utecht's NFL career as a tight end began in 2004 and ended in 2009 when he was injured during training camp with Cincinnati. He was part of the Indianapolis Colts' Super Bowl XLI win.

NOVEMBER 27

"I just go out there and work as hard as I can for the good of His glory, and the rest is in God's hands."

—MIKE FISHER, NHL CENTER

"Serve wholeheartedly, as if serving the Lord, not people."

—EPHESIANS 6:7

Mike Fisher's life story is told in the book *Defender of Faith* by Kim Washburn. It is available through Zonderkidz.

FEBRUARY 5

"Do you have a friend
who needs encouragement
from you today?"

—SHANE DOAN, NHL ALL-STAR RIGHT WING

"Speaking the truth in love, we will grow to
become in every respect the mature body
of him who is the head, that is, Christ."

—EPHESIANS 4:15

Through the 2013–2014 season, Shane Doan's career points total
(goals and assists) put him in the top 125 of all-time in NHL history.

NOVEMBER 26

"God has put us right where we are for a reason, so don't worry about the future."

—CASEY SHAW, PRO BASKETBALL PLAYER

" 'For I know the plans I have for you,' declares the Lord, 'plans to prosper you and not to harm you, plans to give you a hope and a future.' "

—JEREMIAH 29:11

Casey Shaw had a 13-year career in pro basketball, both in the NBA and overseas.

FEBRUARY 6

"In the end,
I want Jesus Christ to
be honored and glorified."

—CHRIS KAMAN, NBA ALL-STAR CENTER

"That all may honor the Son just as they honor
the Father. Whoever does not honor the Son
does not honor the Father, who sent him."

—JOHN 5:23

Chris Kaman attended Central Michigan University and was a first-round NBA draft
pick in 2003. He played for the LA Clippers, New Orleans, Dallas, and the LA Lakers.

NOVEMBER 25

"I pray that people will ask for forgiveness and turn to God, and that we will truly love our neighbor."

—DIKEMBE MUTOMBO, NBA ALL-STAR CENTER

"Bear with each other and forgive one another if any of you has a grievance against someone. Forgive as the Lord forgave you."

—COLOSSIANS 3:13

Raised in the Democratic Republic of the Congo, Dikembe Mutombo enjoyed an 18-year NBA career. In 2007 he opened the Biamba Marie Mutombo Hospital that he founded and funded.

FEBRUARY
7

"Like the tree that flourishes in a drought, the godly person who delights in God's Word can survive a spiritual desert as well."

—CASEY SHAW, PRO BASKETBALL PLAYER

"You will seek me and find me when you seek me with all your heart."

—JEREMIAH 29:13

Casey Shaw enjoyed a 13-year career in pro basketball, both in the NBA and overseas. He and his wife, Dana Drew, both played college hoops at the University of Toledo.

NOVEMBER 24

"Being successful is nice, but it doesn't necessarily bring you happiness. Loving God, studying the Bible—that does."

—TOM LEHMAN, PGA GOLFER

"Oh, how I love your law!
I meditate on it all day long."

—PSALM 119:97

Tom Lehman won five PGA Tour championships during his long and distinguished career, including the 1996 British Open.

FEBRUARY
8

"No matter what your lot is in life, take a moment to think about all the blessings in your life."

—LEIGHANN DOAN REIMER, CANADIAN BASKETBALL PLAYER

"I have learned the secret of being content in any and every situation."

—PHILIPPIANS 4:12

Canadian basketball star Leighann Doan Reimer was a member of the Canadian national teams in 2002 and 2003.

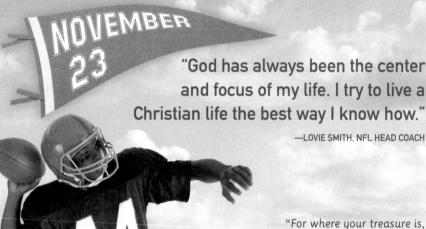

NOVEMBER 23

"God has always been the center and focus of my life. I try to live a Christian life the best way I know how."

—LOVIE SMITH, NFL HEAD COACH

"For where your treasure is, there your heart will be also."

—LUKE 12:34

After being fired by the Chicago Bears after leading them to a Super Bowl and a record of 81–63, Lovie Smith was hired in 2014 to be the head coach of the Tampa Bay Buccaneers.

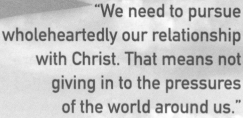

FEBRUARY 9

"We need to pursue wholeheartedly our relationship with Christ. That means not giving in to the pressures of the world around us."

—SARA HALL, LONG-DISTANCE RUNNER

"Do not conform to the pattern of this world, but be transformed by the renewing of your mind."

—ROMANS 12:2

In 2012 Sara Hall won the gold medal in the steeplechase at the Pan American Games in Guadalajara, Mexico. Her husband is fellow runner Ryan Hall.

NOVEMBER 22

"My prayer every day is that I can be a light somewhere, so that someone says, 'Tell me a little bit about Jesus Christ.'"

—MARK JACKSON, NBA ALL-STAR GUARD AND HEAD COACH

"For you were once darkness, but now you are light in the Lord. Live as children of light."

—EPHESIANS 5:8

Known now for his coaching of the Golden State Warriors, Mark Jackson spent 17 years in the NBA. He dished out 10,334 assists, which is third best in NBA history.

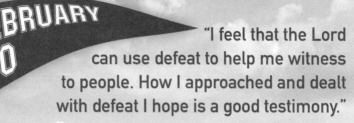

FEBRUARY 10

"I feel that the Lord can use defeat to help me witness to people. How I approached and dealt with defeat I hope is a good testimony."

—CAROLINE LALIVE, OLYMPIC SKIER

"[Jesus said,] 'Whoever wants to be my disciple must deny themselves and take up their cross and follow me. For whoever wants to save their life will lose it, but whoever loses their life for me and for the gospel will save it.' "

—MARK 8:34–35

Caroline Lalive competed for the USA in alpine skiing in both the 1998 and 2002 Winter Olympics.

"Enjoy the freedom that comes from knowing that God is in control. And have a servant's heart—put others first."

—SHANE DOAN, NHL ALL-STAR RIGHT WING

"You, my brothers and sisters, were called to be free. But do not use your freedom to indulge the flesh; rather, serve one another humbly in love."

—GALATIANS 5:13

Shane Doan was a member of Canada's Winter Olympic team in 2006.

FEBRUARY
11

"We all need a Savior. He can give us the eternal life we don't deserve."

—HERSEY HAWKINS, NBA ALL-STAR GUARD

"For all have sinned and fall short of the glory of God."

—ROMANS 3:23

Only six players in NCAA history scored more points than Bradley University's Hersey Hawkins. He tallied 3,008 points, including an average of 36 points a game as a senior.

NOVEMBER 20

"What an example of grace Jesus bought for us on the cross! We were guilty, but Jesus shed His blood so our sins could be washed away."

—BOB CHRISTIAN, NFL FULLBACK

"For I will forgive their wickedness and will remember their sins no more."

—HEBREWS 8:12

In his best year in the NFL, Bob Christian rushed for 284 yards and two TDs and caught 45 passes for 392 yards and two TDs for the Atlanta Falcons.

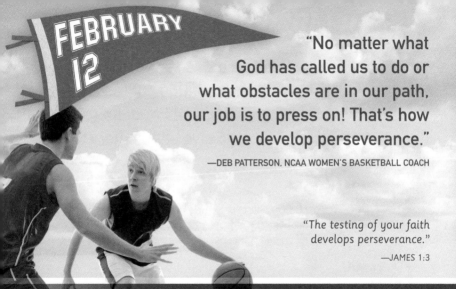

FEBRUARY 12

"No matter what God has called us to do or what obstacles are in our path, our job is to press on! That's how we develop perseverance."

—DEB PATTERSON, NCAA WOMEN'S BASKETBALL COACH

"The testing of your faith develops perseverance."

—JAMES 1:3

As women's basketball coach at Kansas State, Deb Patterson has sent at least seven of her players to the WNBA.

NOVEMBER 19

"You've got to stand up and make sacrifices, decisions, and choices. God put me here for a reason, and I'm definitely going to give all the glory to Him."

—COLT MCCOY, NFL QUARTERBACK

"Therefore, preparing your minds for action, and being sober-minded, set your hope fully on the grace that will be brought to you at the revelation of Jesus Christ."

—1 PETER 1:13 (ENGLISH STANDARD VERSION)

While playing quarterback for the University of Texas, Colt McCoy was named the 2009 AT&T ESPN All-America Player of the Year.

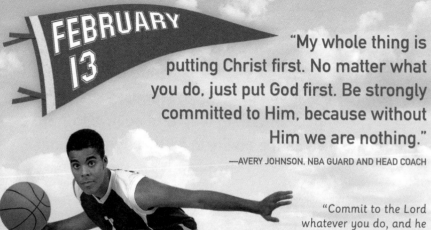

FEBRUARY 13

"My whole thing is putting Christ first. No matter what you do, just put God first. Be strongly committed to Him, because without Him we are nothing."

—AVERY JOHNSON, NBA GUARD AND HEAD COACH

"Commit to the Lord whatever you do, and he will establish your plans."

—PROVERBS 16:3

In his first seven seasons as an NBA coach, Avery Johnson's record was 254–186, a .577 win percentage.

NOVEMBER 18

"It's not our job to try to sit back and pick what God is going to do next. We just have to trust Him and walk in faith and believe that He's going to give us the ability to go through all things."

—KEVIN OLLIE, NBA FORWARD AND COLLEGE HEAD COACH

"For we live by faith, not by sight."

—2 CORINTHIANS 5:7

In 2012 Kevin Ollie was named the head coach at the University of Connecticut.

FEBRUARY 14

"When things go bad, we have a tendency to shy away from faith. But Jesus Christ has a plan. As bad as things may look now, we know that there's a brighter picture tomorrow."

—HERSEY HAWKINS, NBA ALL-STAR GUARD

"The Lord is my strength and my shield; my heart trusts in him, and he helps me."

—PSALM 28:7

During his NBA career, Hersey Hawkins scored 14,470 points, including hitting 1,226 three-pointers.

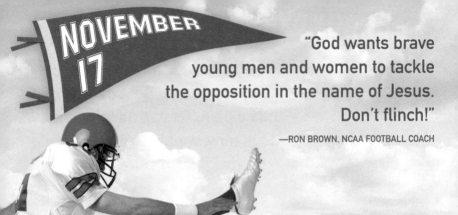

NOVEMBER 17

"God wants brave young men and women to tackle the opposition in the name of Jesus. Don't flinch!"

—RON BROWN, NCAA FOOTBALL COACH

"Be on your guard; stand firm in the faith; be courageous; be strong."

—1 CORINTHIANS 16:13

Nebraska assistant coach Ron Brown has told his life story in the book *I Can*.

FEBRUARY 15

"Only you can speak from your own personal experience. Your greatest sermon is your own life, your personal testimony."

—A. C. GREEN, NBA ALL-STAR FORWARD

"Come and hear, all you who fear God; let me tell you what he has done for me."

—PSALM 66:16

A. C. Green holds the NBA record for most consecutive games played: 1,192 games across 15 seasons.

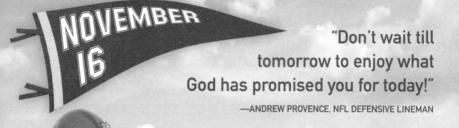

NOVEMBER 16

"Don't wait till tomorrow to enjoy what God has promised you for today!"

—ANDREW PROVENCE, NFL DEFENSIVE LINEMAN

"I have come that they may have life, and have it to the full."

—JOHN 10:10

A former Atlanta Falcon and Denver Bronco, Andrew Provence works with Athletes in Action.

"Your quiet time with God is so important. Whenever I get too busy and get away from taking my quiet time, it just doesn't seem right. Something's not in balance."

—TONY BENNETT, NBA GUARD AND COLLEGE COACH

"But when you pray, go into your room, close the door and pray to your Father, who is unseen. Then your Father, who sees what is done in secret, will reward you."

—MATTHEW 6:6

After graduating from the University of Wisconsin–Green Bay, Tony Bennett spent three seasons in the NBA with the Charlotte Hornets.

"I'm a big fan of the parable of the talents that Jesus told. It is our responsibility to use the talents God has given us and to multiply them for the glory of God."

—STEFEN WISNIEWSKI, NFL OFFENSIVE LINEMAN

"Whoever has will be given more, and they will have an abundance. Whoever does not have, even what they have will be taken from them."

—MATTHEW 25:29

While playing with the Raiders, Stefan Wisniewski was named to the 2011 All-Rookie team by the *Sporting News*.

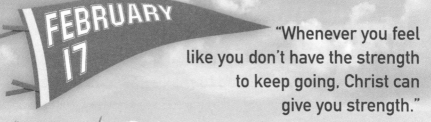

FEBRUARY 17

"Whenever you feel like you don't have the strength to keep going, Christ can give you strength."

—CHARLIE WARD, NBA GUARD AND HIGH SCHOOL FOOTBALL COACH

"For the Lord your God is the one who goes with you to fight for you against your enemies to give you victory."

—DEUTERONOMY 20:4

Charlie Ward won the 1993 Heisman Trophy as quarterback at Florida State University. He also played basketball at FSU all four years.

NOVEMBER 14

"What things are you asking God to make possible for you?"

—DEB PATTERSON, NCAA WOMEN'S BASKETBALL COACH

"God is able to bless you abundantly."

—2 CORINTHIANS 9:8

During her tenure at Kansas State, Deb Patterson has led the Wildcats to more than 350 victories.

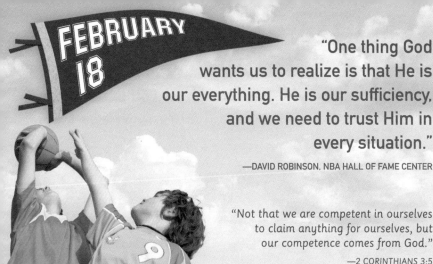

FEBRUARY 18

"One thing God wants us to realize is that He is our everything. He is our sufficiency, and we need to trust Him in every situation."

—DAVID ROBINSON, NBA HALL OF FAME CENTER

"Not that we are competent in ourselves to claim anything for ourselves, but our competence comes from God."

—2 CORINTHIANS 3:5

On April 24, 1994, David Robinson scored 71 points for the San Antonio Spurs in a win over the Los Angeles Clippers.

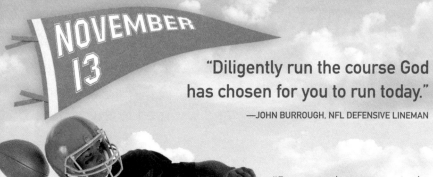

NOVEMBER 13

"Diligently run the course God has chosen for you to run today."

—JOHN BURROUGH, NFL DEFENSIVE LINEMAN

"Everyone who competes in the games goes into strict training. They do it to get a crown that will not last, but we do it to get a crown that will last forever."

—1 CORINTHIANS 9:25

After John Burrough's six-year NFL career ended, he began building custom homes in the Atlanta area: Nehemiah Custom Homes. He is active with Fellowship of Christian Athletes.

FEBRUARY 19

"Hang around other believers. I think they can encourage you and show you the right way. Find good Christian friends, and do things with them."

—BRYCE DREW, NBA GUARD AND COLLEGE COACH

"Do not be misled: 'Bad company corrupts good character.' "

—1 CORINTHIANS 15:33

The Houston Rockets drafted Bryce Drew out of Valparaiso University.
He played six years in the NBA and scored just over 1,000 points.

NOVEMBER 12

"I prepare for victory by knowing my God and protecting myself against the enemy."

—KYLE BRADY, NFL TIGHT END

"My help comes from the Lord, the Maker of heaven and earth."

—PSALM 121:2

After his NFL career ended, Kyle Brady became a lawyer and a licensed financial advisor.

"If you put yourself in a tempting situation, probably nine times out of ten you're going to muff it. The key is to put yourself in situations where you won't fall."

—HUBERT DAVIS, NBA GUARD AND COLLEGE COACH

"No temptation has overtaken you except what is common to mankind. And God is faithful; he will not let you be tempted beyond what you can bear. But when you are tempted, he will also provide a way out so that you can endure it."

—1 CORINTHIANS 10:13

During the 1999–2000 NBA season, Hubert Davis led the league in three-point shooting percentage. He hit .491 percent of his long-range shots (82 for 167).

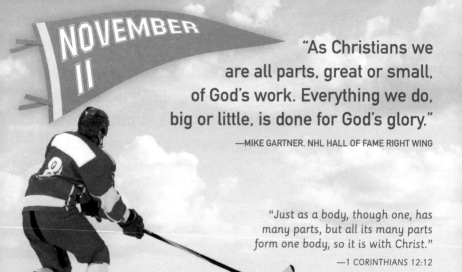

NOVEMBER 11

"As Christians we are all parts, great or small, of God's work. Everything we do, big or little, is done for God's glory."

—MIKE GARTNER, NHL HALL OF FAME RIGHT WING

"Just as a body, though one, has many parts, but all its many parts form one body, so it is with Christ."

—1 CORINTHIANS 12:12

Mike Gartner was elected to the Hockey Hall of Fame in 2001 after a playing career that extended from 1978 until 1998.

FEBRUARY 21

"You're going to have trials. You're going to be tested. The one thing God has promised is victory in the end. But He never promised we would be ahead at halftime."

—JOE CARTER, MLB ALL-STAR OUTFIELDER

"I know that my redeemer lives, and that in the end he will stand on the earth."

—JOB 19:25

Joe Carter hit a home run to give the Toronto Blue Jays a walk-off, seventh-game victory in the 1993 World Series, making the Blue Jays back-to-back world champions.

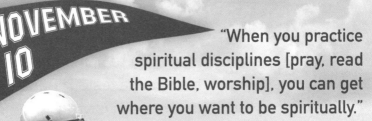

NOVEMBER 10

"When you practice spiritual disciplines [pray, read the Bible, worship], you can get where you want to be spiritually."

—KIRK COUSINS, NFL QUARTERBACK

"Let the message of Christ dwell among you richly as you teach and admonish one another with all wisdom through psalms, hymns, and songs from the Spirit, singing to God with gratitude in your hearts."

—COLOSSIANS 3:16

In his final game for Michigan State, Kirk Cousins led the Spartans past the Georgia Bulldogs in the Outback Bowl.

FEBRUARY 22

"You have to keep your focus on Christ and try to get into His Word as often as you can."

—GARY CARTER, MLB HALL OF FAME CATCHER

"I have hidden your word in my heart that I might not sin against you."

—PSALM 119:11

Gary Carter (1954–2012) was inducted into the National Baseball Hall of Fame in Cooperstown in 2003.

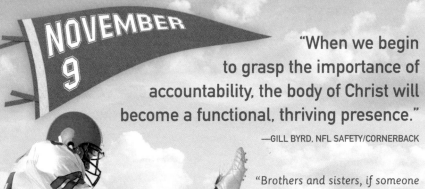

NOVEMBER 9

"When we begin to grasp the importance of accountability, the body of Christ will become a functional, thriving presence."

—GILL BYRD, NFL SAFETY/CORNERBACK

"Brothers and sisters, if someone is caught in a sin, you who live by the Spirit should restore that person gently. But watch yourselves, or you may also be tempted."

—GALATIANS 6:1

During his distinguished NFL career from 1983 through 1992, Gill Byrd intercepted 42 passes. In 1984 he picked off one pass and returned the ball 99 yards for a touchdown.

FEBRUARY 23

"Stay in prayer.
Through spending time
getting to know God's heart,
I can deal with things."

—HAROLD REYNOLDS, MLB ALL-STAR INFIELDER,
TV BASEBALL ANALYST

"Look to the Lord and his strength;
seek his face always."

—1 CHRONICLES 16:11

Harold Reynolds was an All-Star infielder for the Seattle Mariners
(1987, 1988). In 1987 he led the league in stolen bases with 60.

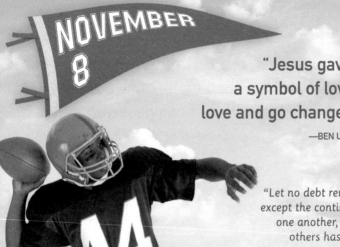

NOVEMBER 8

"Jesus gave His life as a symbol of love. Take that love and go change the world."

—BEN UTECHT, NFL TIGHT END

"Let no debt remain outstanding, except the continuing debt to love one another, for whoever loves others has fulfilled the law."

—ROMANS 13:8

During Ben Utecht's injury-shortened NFL career, he caught 87 passes for 923 yards and three touchdowns for Indianapolis and Cincinnati.

FEBRUARY 24

"You look at pro athletes, and it seems that they have everything—cars, wealth, fame—but really, we have nothing unless we have Christ."

—JASON HANSON, NFL KICKER

"No one can serve two masters. Either you will hate the one and love the other, or you will be devoted to the one and despise the other. You cannot serve both God and money."

—MATTHEW 6:24

When Jason Hanson retired after the 2012 NFL season, he had accumulated 2,150 points in his kicking career for the Detroit Lions.

NOVEMBER 7

"If we really want to be more like Jesus, we have to train ourselves—spend time in God's Word, pray, use self-control. Spiritual training takes holy sweat."

—KEN MOYER, NFL LINEMAN

"Physical training is of some value, but godliness has value for all things, holding promise for both the present life and the life to come."

—1 TIMOTHY 4:8

Ken Moyer played college football at the University of Toledo, and then he played in the NFL with the Cincinnati Bengals as an offensive lineman.

FEBRUARY 25

"I just want to try to be a good example whether I'm on or off the field. If I can do that and lead others to Christ, then I'll be successful."

—TIM TEBOW, NFL QUARTERBACK, ESPN ANALYST

"Set an example for the believers in speech, in conduct, in love, in faith and in purity."

—1 TIMOTHY 4:12

Tim Tebow, who was homeschooled in high school, won the Heisman Trophy in 2007 as the best player in college football.

NOVEMBER 6

"How can you best pray for your home— and friends not in your home—today?"

—JESSICA WUERFFEL, WIFE OF NFL QUARTERBACK DANNY WUERFFEL

"Seek the peace and prosperity of the city to which I have carried you into exile. Pray to the Lord for it, because if it prospers, you too will prosper."

—JEREMIAH 29:7

Calvin College graduate Jessica Wuerffel teams up with her husband, Danny, a former NFL quarterback, to serve kids in the inner city of New Orleans through Desire Street Ministries.

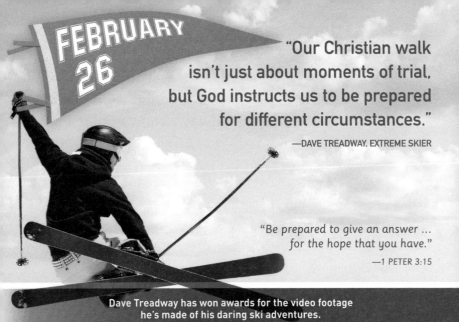

FEBRUARY 26

"Our Christian walk isn't just about moments of trial, but God instructs us to be prepared for different circumstances."

—DAVE TREADWAY, EXTREME SKIER

"Be prepared to give an answer ... for the hope that you have."

—1 PETER 3:15

Dave Treadway has won awards for the video footage he's made of his daring ski adventures.

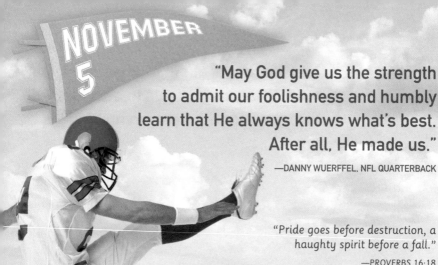

NOVEMBER 5

"May God give us the strength to admit our foolishness and humbly learn that He always knows what's best. After all, He made us."

—DANNY WUERFFEL, NFL QUARTERBACK

"Pride goes before destruction, a haughty spirit before a fall."

—PROVERBS 16:18

In 1996 Danny Wuerffel won the Heisman Trophy for his efforts as quarterback at the University of Florida. In the NFL he played for New Orleans, Green Bay, Chicago, and Washington.

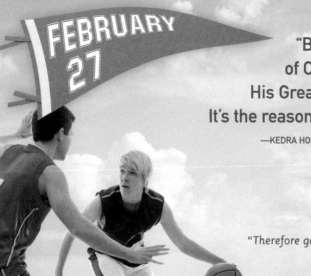

FEBRUARY 27

"Be an extension
of Christ and fulfill
His Great Commission.
It's the reason you are here."

—KEDRA HOLLAND-CORN, WNBA GUARD

"Therefore go and make disciples."

—MATTHEW 28:19

Kedra Holland-Corn won a gold medal while playing for the
US team in the 1997 World University Games in Sicily, Italy.

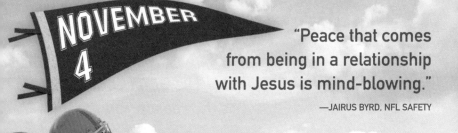

NOVEMBER 4

"Peace that comes from being in a relationship with Jesus is mind-blowing."

—JAIRUS BYRD, NFL SAFETY

"Cast all your anxiety on him because he cares for you."

—1 PETER 5:7

Jairus Byrd was selected for the Pro Bowl in three of his first five seasons in the NFL.

FEBRUARY 28

"We as Christians are called to be humble. And if we really understand the gospel, we *will* be humble."

—JEREMY LIN, NBA GUARD

"Be completely humble and gentle; be patient, bearing with one another in love."

—EPHESIANS 4:2

Jeremy Lin averaged 13 points a game while an undergraduate at Harvard University (2006–2010).

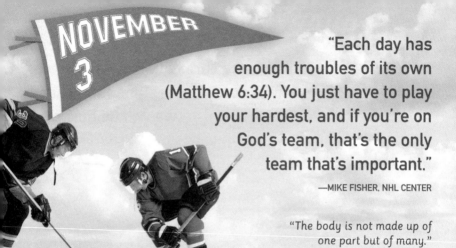

NOVEMBER 3

"Each day has enough troubles of its own (Matthew 6:34). You just have to play your hardest, and if you're on God's team, that's the only team that's important."

—MIKE FISHER, NHL CENTER

"The body is not made up of one part but of many."

—1 CORINTHIANS 12:14

Mike Fisher's highest scoring NHL season was 2009–2010 when he scored 53 points (25 goals; 28 assists) for the Ottawa Senators.

FEBRUARY 29

"Trust that God will strengthen you as you run the race. You must not quit."

—VALERIE STERK KEMPER,
US NATIONAL VOLLEYBALL PLAYER

"Finally, be strong in the Lord
and in his mighty power."

—EPHESIANS 6:10

After an All-American career on the volleyball court at Michigan State University,
Valerie was a member of the US National team in 2000.

"Your testimony is louder when you're going through hard times. It's easy when everything is going your way. The true test of a person is who they are during those difficult times."

—MATT HASSELBECK, NFL QUARTERBACK

"In all this you greatly rejoice, though now for a little while you may have had to suffer grief in all kinds of trials. These have come so that the proven genuineness of your faith—of greater worth than gold, which perishes even though refined by fire—may result in praise, glory and honor when Jesus Christ is revealed."

—1 PETER 1:6–7

Matt Hasselbeck's long and distinguished NFL career began in 1998 with Green Bay. He is the all-time Seattle Seahawks' passing leader with 29,434 yards.

MARCH 1

"I always try to give God all the glory."

—ALLYSON FELIX,
OLYMPIC GOLD MEDAL–WINNING SPRINTER

"Sing to the Lord a new song; sing to the Lord, all the earth. Sing to the Lord, praise his name; proclaim his salvation day after day."

—PSALM 96:1–2

A graduate of Los Angeles Baptist High School, Allyson Felix received the Best Female Track Athlete ESPY Award in 2006.

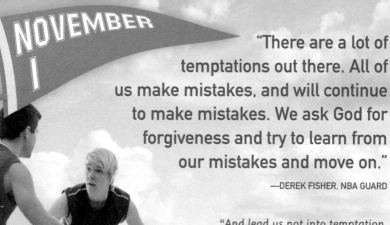

NOVEMBER 1

"There are a lot of temptations out there. All of us make mistakes, and will continue to make mistakes. We ask God for forgiveness and try to learn from our mistakes and move on."

—DEREK FISHER, NBA GUARD

"And lead us not into temptation, but deliver us from the evil one."

—MATTHEW 6:13

During his NBA career, Derek Fisher won five NBA championships while with the LA Lakers.

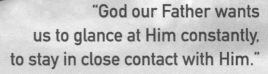

MARCH 2

"God our Father wants us to glance at Him constantly, to stay in close contact with Him."

—SUE SEMRAU, NCAA BASKETBALL COACH

"Turn my heart toward your statutes and not toward selfish gain. Turn my eyes away from worthless things; preserve my life according to your word."

—PSALM 119:36–37

In 2013 Sue Semrau won the Kay Yow Heart of a Coach Award, an honor bestowed by the Fellowship of Christian Athletes.

OCTOBER 31

"Peace comes from the Lord.
It's a privilege. It's a gift."

—STEVE SMITH, NFL ALL-PRO WIDE RECEIVER

"Now may the Lord of peace
himself give you peace at all
times and in every way.
The Lord be with all of you."

—2 THESSALONIANS 3:16

In 2005 Steve Smith was voted NFL Comeback Player of the Year.
He led the league in receiving TDs that season.

MARCH 3

"Memorize Scripture, then when trials come we can defeat the enemy with the Word of God."

—TANYA CREVIER,
BASKETBALL BALL-HANDLING EXPERT

"For the word of the Lord is right and true; he is faithful in all he does."

—PSALM 33:4

Tanya Crevier spent three years in the Women's Pro Basketball League (WBL), but she makes her mark as a traveling basketball show person who shares her unbelievable ball-handling skills all over the Western Hemisphere.

OCTOBER 30

"I'm a Christian and I believe in God. And when you do great, you stay humble and you give Him glory."

—NICK FOLES, NFL QUARTERBACK

"Better to be lowly in spirit along with the oppressed than to share plunder with the proud."

—PROVERBS 16:19

Nick Foles enjoyed what is considered a perfect game for a quarterback (158.3 passer rating) on November 3, 2013. He was 22 for 28 in passing for 406 yards and seven touchdowns.

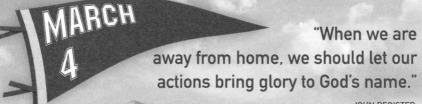

MARCH 4

"When we are away from home, we should let our actions bring glory to God's name."

—JOHN REGISTER,
PARALYMPIC MEDAL WINNER

"Let them give glory to the Lord and proclaim his praise."

—ISAIAH 42:12

In 2000 John Register won a silver medal in the long jump at the Paralympic Games. In 1996 he competed in the Paralympics in swimming.

"God invites us to be forgiven of all sin and to receive eternal life, not by trying to do good works, but by trusting in Jesus as Lord and Savior. Salvation is a free gift of God."

—DAVID AKERS, NFL ALL-PRO KICKER

"For the wages of sin is death, but the gift of God is eternal life in Christ Jesus our Lord."

—ROMANS 6:23

A six-time Pro Bowl selection, David Akers holds the NFL record for most points in a season by a kicker (166). He also holds the mark for most field goals in a season (44).

MARCH 5

"What a difference it makes to think about God's power, love, and grace through song rather than having songs about the things of the world floating through my head."

—BARB LINDQUIST, OLYMPIC TRIATHLETE

"Come, let us sing for joy to the Lord; let us shout aloud to the Rock of our salvation."

—PSALM 95:1

In 2003 Barb Lindquist was the No. 1 ranked women's triathlete in the world. In 2007 she and her husband, Loren, had twin boys: Bjorn and Zane.

OCTOBER 28

"Study the armor of God in Ephesians 6:12–17. Put it on every day."

—SHANE DOAN,
NHL ALL-STAR RIGHT WING

"Put on the full armor of God."

—EPHESIANS 6:13

Since starting with Winnipeg (now Phoenix) in 1995, Shane Doan has played in more than 1,300 games for the same team.

MARCH
6

"God knows we will get angry. He created us with that emotion, but what we do with it is our decision. With His help, we can keep it under control."

—DEEDEE JONROWE, IDITAROD MUSHER

"Fools give full vent to their rage, but the wise bring calm in the end."

—PROVERBS 29:11

DeeDee Jonrowe first raced the Iditarod trail in the "Last Great Race on Earth" in 1980 and has been racing in them ever since. In 1998 she finished second in the Anchorage to Nome dogsled race.

OCTOBER 27

"I always want to tweak or improve the way I do things. That's kind of the attitude I take into reading the Bible or living for Christ."

—BILL MUELLER, MLB THIRD BASEMAN

"For the word of God is living and active. Sharper than any double-edged sword, it penetrates even to dividing soul and spirit, ... it judges the thoughts and attitudes of the heart."

—HEBREWS 4:12

Most famous for his contributions to the Boston Red Sox when they won the 2004 World Series, Bill Mueller was a major leaguer from 1996 until 2006. He had a career batting average of .291, and he won the AL batting title in 2003.

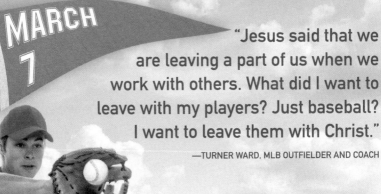

MARCH
7

"Jesus said that we are leaving a part of us when we work with others. What did I want to leave with my players? Just baseball? I want to leave them with Christ."

—TURNER WARD, MLB OUTFIELDER AND COACH

"The student is not above the teacher, but everyone who is fully trained will be like their teacher."

—LUKE 6:40

Turner Ward's 12-year career as an outfielder ended in 2001, after which he got into coaching. He was hired as a coach with the Arizona Diamondbacks in 2013.

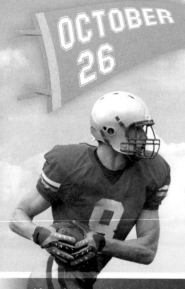

OCTOBER 26

"When we accept God's free gift of forgiveness through Christ, our sins are washed away. God, through Jesus, forgives us."

—BOB CHRISTIAN, NFL RUNNING BACK

"In Christ Jesus you who once were far away have been brought near by the blood of Christ."

—EPHESIANS 2:13

After playing at Northwestern University, Bob Christian spent 10 years in the NFL as a running back for the Chicago Bears, the Carolina Panthers, and the Atlanta Falcons.

MARCH
8

"Take some time to formulate your story of faith in Jesus. Then tell it to others."

—PAUL GRAFER, MLS GOALKEEPER

"How, then, can they call on the one they have not believed in? And how can they believe in the one of whom they have not heard?"

—ROMANS 10:14

Paul Grafer played for Colorado and the MetroStars in Major League Soccer. After he retired, he became a coach for the US U-17s.

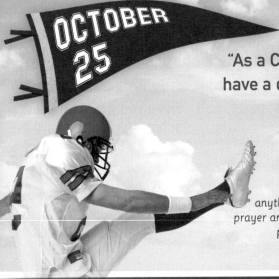

OCTOBER 25

"As a Christian, you always have a different perspective than the world has."

—TONY DUNGY, NFL DEFENSIVE BACK, QUARTERBACK, AND HEAD COACH

"Do not be anxious about anything, but in every situation, by prayer and petition, with thanksgiving, present your requests to God."

—PHILIPPIANS 4:6

Since the late 1960s, only one person has thrown an interception and intercepted a pass in the same game: Tony Dungy. He did it in a game between Pittsburgh and the Houston Oilers in 1977.

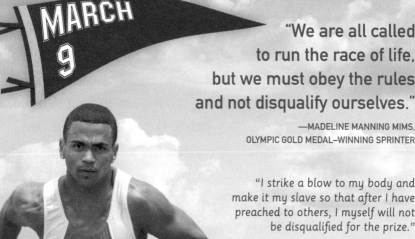

MARCH 9

"We are all called to run the race of life, but we must obey the rules and not disqualify ourselves."

—MADELINE MANNING MIMS,
OLYMPIC GOLD MEDAL–WINNING SPRINTER

"I strike a blow to my body and make it my slave so that after I have preached to others, I myself will not be disqualified for the prize."

—1 CORINTHIANS 9:27

Madeline Manning was part of the US track team in the Summer Olympics of 1968, 1972, and 1976. She won both a gold and a silver medal during her Olympic career as a sprinter.

OCTOBER 24

"You can say, 'Why is this happening to me?' But you have to understand that it's happening for a reason, and God is doing it to strengthen you."

—DREW BREES, NFL ALL-PRO QUARTERBACK

"The God of all grace, who called you to his eternal glory in Christ, after you have suffered a little while, will himself restore you and make you strong, firm and steadfast."

—1 PETER 5:10

Drew Brees was named the MVP of Super Bowl XLIV after leading the New Orleans Saints to victory.

MARCH 10

"Appearances can be deceiving; Jesus encourages us to seek knowledge and obtain truth."

—DAVID THOMPSON, NBA HALL OF FAME FORWARD

"If we claim to have fellowship with him and yet walk in darkness, we lie and do not live out the truth."

—1 JOHN 1:6

David Thompson was an All-Star in both the ABA and the NBA. The Denver Nuggets retired his number, 33.

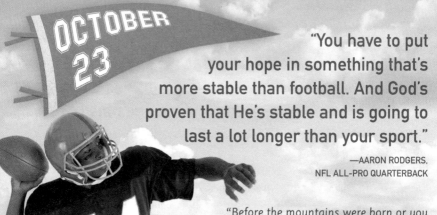

OCTOBER 23

"You have to put your hope in something that's more stable than football. And God's proven that He's stable and is going to last a lot longer than your sport."

—AARON RODGERS,
NFL ALL-PRO QUARTERBACK

"Before the mountains were born or you brought forth the whole world, from everlasting to everlasting you are God."

—PSALM 90:2

In 2011 Aaron Rodgers was named the MVP of the NFL. He led the Green Bay Packers to victory in Super Bowl XLV and was named the game's MVP.

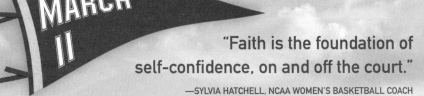

MARCH 11

"Faith is the foundation of self-confidence, on and off the court."

—SYLVIA HATCHELL, NCAA WOMEN'S BASKETBALL COACH

"We say with confidence,
'The Lord is my helper;
I will not be afraid. What can
mere mortals do to me?'"

—HEBREWS 13:6

Sylvia Hatchell has won 900 games as a college basketball coach, mostly at North Carolina. She was national Coach of the Year in 1994 and 2006.

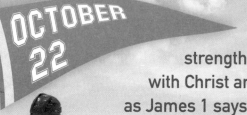

OCTOBER 22

"The source of my strength is my relationship with Christ and in knowing that, as James 1 says, through my trials I should have patience and that the Lord is perfect in His timing."

—JOHN VANBIESBROUCK, NHL GOALIE

"Let perseverance finish its work so that you may be mature and complete, not lacking anything."

—JAMES 1:4

John VanBiesbrouck was an NHL goalie from 1981 until 2002. He was inducted into the United States Hockey Hall of Fame in 2007. In 2013 he became the GM of a team in the US Hockey League, the Muskegon (MI) Lumberjacks.

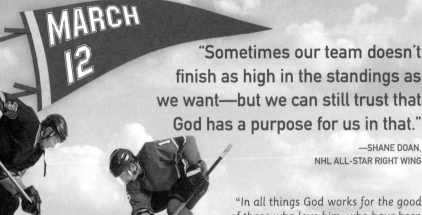

MARCH 12

"Sometimes our team doesn't finish as high in the standings as we want—but we can still trust that God has a purpose for us in that."

—SHANE DOAN,
NHL ALL-STAR RIGHT WING

"In all things God works for the good of those who love him, who have been called according to his purpose."

—ROMANS 8:28

Shane Doan was the winner of the Elimination Shootout at the 2009 NHL All-Star Game.

OCTOBER 21

"As a Christian, it's easy to get caught up in the pleasures of the world. Don't get caught in that trap!"

—GILL BYRD, NFL SAFETY/CORNERBACK

"If anyone, then, knows the good they ought to do and doesn't do it, it is sin for them."

—JAMES 4:17

Since Gill Byrd's 10-year NFL career ended, he has coached for the Bears, Rams, and Buccaneers.

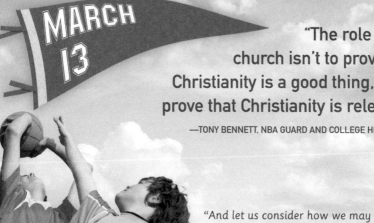

MARCH 13

"The role of the church isn't to prove that Christianity is a good thing, it's to prove that Christianity is relevant."

—TONY BENNETT, NBA GUARD AND COLLEGE HEAD COACH

"And let us consider how we may spur one another on toward love and good deeds."

—HEBREWS 10:24

Tony Bennett was named the 2007 Naismith College Coach of the Year for his efforts at Washington State.

OCTOBER 20

"The truth is, contentment is found in Christ alone."

—MATT STOVER. NFL ALL-PRO KICKER

"But now, Lord, what do I look for?
My hope is in you."

—PSALM 39:7

**Kicker Matt Stover was a member of two
Super Bowl-winning teams (XXV 1991, XXXV 2001).**

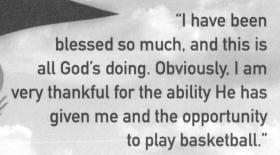

MARCH 14

"I have been blessed so much, and this is all God's doing. Obviously, I am very thankful for the ability He has given me and the opportunity to play basketball."

—CHRIS PAUL, NBA ALL-STAR GUARD

"All these are the work of one and the same Spirit, and he distributes them to each one, just as he determines."

—1 CORINTHIANS 12:11

Chris Paul was voted the MVP of the 2013 NBA All-Star Game.

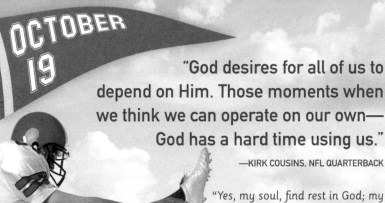

OCTOBER 19

"God desires for all of us to depend on Him. Those moments when we think we can operate on our own— God has a hard time using us."

—KIRK COUSINS, NFL QUARTERBACK

"Yes, my soul, find rest in God; my hope comes from him. Truly he is my rock and my salvation; he is my fortress, I will not be shaken."

—PSALM 62:5–6

While at Michigan State University, Kirk Cousins set school records for passing touchdowns (66), passing yards (9,131), and passing efficiency (146.1 passer rating).

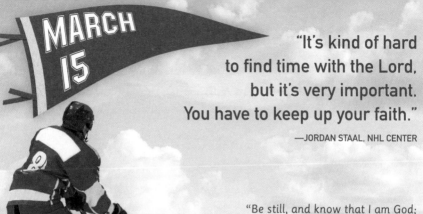

MARCH 15

"It's kind of hard to find time with the Lord, but it's very important. You have to keep up your faith."

—JORDAN STAAL, NHL CENTER

"Be still, and know that I am God; I will be exalted among the nations, I will be exalted in the earth."

—PSALM 46:10

Jordan Staal has three brothers who also have played in the NHL: Eric, Jared, and Marc.

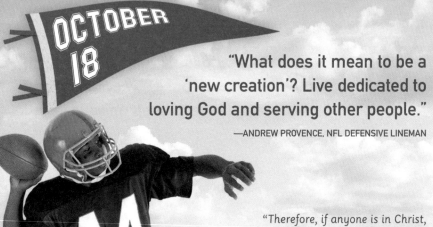

OCTOBER 18

"What does it mean to be a 'new creation'? Live dedicated to loving God and serving other people."

—ANDREW PROVENCE, NFL DEFENSIVE LINEMAN

"Therefore, if anyone is in Christ, the new creation has come."

—2 CORINTHIANS 5:17

After finishing his NFL career with Atlanta and Denver, Andrew Provence became a professional counselor so he could help people going through hard times.

MARCH 16

"Life is not a sprint; it is an endurance race. With God's grace we can clear away the weight that slows us down— physically and spiritually."

—DEEDEE JONROWE, IDITAROD MUSHER

"Let us throw off everything that hinders and the sin that so easily entangles. And let us run with perseverance the race marked out for us."

—HEBREWS 12:1

Iditarod musher DeeDee Jonrowe battled cancer, beat it, and continued to race. DeeDee and her husband, Mike, live in Willow, Alaska.

OCTOBER 17

"Gain a vision for your life by trusting God's plan."

—JEREMY AFFELDT, MLB PITCHER

"Where there is no revelation, people cast off restraint."

—PROVERBS 29:18

In 2013 Jeremy Affeldt published a book called *To Stir a Movement*, which helped to introduce some of his important social justice work.

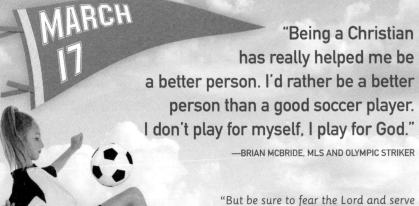

MARCH 17

"Being a Christian has really helped me be a better person. I'd rather be a better person than a good soccer player. I don't play for myself, I play for God."

—BRIAN MCBRIDE, MLS AND OLYMPIC STRIKER

"But be sure to fear the Lord and serve him faithfully with all your heart; consider what great things he has done for you."

—1 SAMUEL 12:24

Brian McBride was a member of the US Olympic soccer team for the 2008 Games.

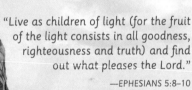

OCTOBER 16

"Let the light of Jesus shine in the way you live each day. People will notice."

—JON KITNA, NFL QUARTERBACK

"Live as children of light (for the fruit of the light consists in all goodness, righteousness and truth) and find out what pleases the Lord."

—EPHESIANS 5:8–10

Jon Kitna was the MVP of the World Bowl in 1997 while with the Barcelona Dragons. He played in the NFL from 1996 until 2011.

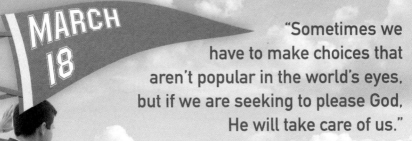

MARCH 18

"Sometimes we have to make choices that aren't popular in the world's eyes, but if we are seeking to please God, He will take care of us."

—ERIN BUESCHER PERPEROGLOU, WNBA FORWARD

"Daniel resolved not to defile himself with the royal food and wine. ... At the end of the ten days [he and his friends] looked healthier and better nourished than any of the young men who ate the royal food."

—DANIEL 1:8

While at The Master's College as a senior, Erin Buescher was named an NAIA All-American and the National Christian College Athletic Association (NCCAA) Player of the Year.

OCTOBER 15

"Have you repented and turned your life over to God?"

—NAPOLEON KAUFMAN, NFL RUNNING BACK

"He saved us, not because of righteous things we had done, but because of his mercy. He saved us through the washing of rebirth and renewal by the Holy Spirit."

—TITUS 3:5

Napoleon Kaufman gained nearly 5,000 yards as an NFL running back for the Oakland Raiders. He retired after the 2000 season at the age of 27 to pursue ministry opportunities.

MARCH 19

"With God's help, you can be victorious. Like Joshua, be strong and courageous."

—WENDY WARD, LPGA GOLFER

"Be strong and very courageous. Be careful to obey all the law."

—JOSHUA 1:7

Wendy Ward represented the United States in the Solheim Cup tournament in 2002, 2003, and 2005. In the Solheim Cup, top golfers from Europe take on top American golfers.

"His blessing may or may not always be manifested in our athletic performances, but it will surely be seen in our relationship with Him!"

—SARA HALL, LONG-DISTANCE RUNNER

"Daniel resolved not to defile himself."

—DANIEL 1:8

In 2012 Sara Hall captured the USA Cross Country championship in St. Louis, Missouri. In 2006 her husband, Ryan Hall, won the men's title in this event.

"Before every game
I will pray just before I go on
the ice. God gave me a special talent,
and I will be forever grateful for that."

—CAM WARD, NHL ALL-STAR GOALIE

"The Lord has done it this very day;
let us rejoice today and be glad."

—PSALM 118:24

On December 26, 2011, Cam Ward became the tenth
NHL goalie in history to record an empty-net goal.

OCTOBER
13

"No matter what happens,
God is with me."

—CLINT GRESHAM, NFL LONG SNAPPER

*"If we love one another, God lives in us
and his love is made complete in us."*

—1 JOHN 4:12

Clint Gresham has played with both the New Orleans Saints and the Seattle
Seahawks. He was a member of the 2014 Super Bowl champion Seahawks.

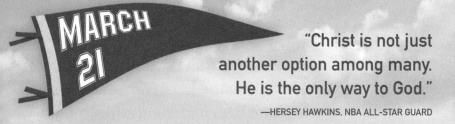

MARCH 21

"Christ is not just another option among many. He is the only way to God."

—HERSEY HAWKINS, NBA ALL-STAR GUARD

"Jesus answered,
'I am the way and
the truth and the life.
No one comes to the
Father except through me.'"

—JOHN 14:6

During his 13-year NBA career, Hersey Hawkins scored 14,470 points, or 14.7 a game in 983 games. He played for Philadelphia, Charlotte, Chicago, and Seattle.

OCTOBER 12

"What is our greatest goal? To love the Lord with all our heart and soul and mind and strength."

—DEB PATTERSON, NCAA WOMEN'S BASKETBALL COACH

"Love the Lord your God with all your heart and with all your soul and with all your mind and with all your strength."

—MARK 12:30

In addition to coaching at Kansas State, Deb Patterson has helped the US Women's National team win gold medals at the World University Games (1997) and the FIBA World Championships (1998).

MARCH 22

"Are you praying, guarding your thoughts, and avoiding Satan's tricks?"

—KATHERINE HULL, LPGA GOLFER

"Be alert and of sober mind. Your enemy the devil prowls around like a roaring lion looking for someone to devour."

—1 PETER 5:8

Katherine graduated from Pepperdine University in 2003 with a degree in Sports Administration. In 2007 she accompanied Betsy King and other golfers on a mission trip to Rwanda.

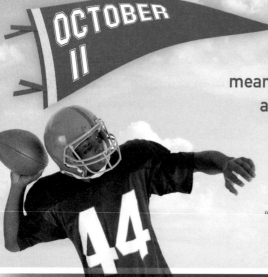

OCTOBER 11

"Sometimes humility means closing your mouth and grinding through."

—BROCK HUARD, NFL QUARTERBACK

"Clothe yourselves with humility toward one another."

—1 PETER 5:5

After a spectacular college career as a quarterback for the University of Washington (5,742 yards passing; 51 passing TDs), Brock Huard had a limited NFL career, throwing just 107 pass attempts.

MARCH 23

"The best investment of our time is to spend it with God."

—KRISTEN SAMP, LPGA GOLFER

"But remember the Lord your God."

—DEUTERONOMY 8:18

As a pro golfer, Kristen Samp's best round on the LPGA circuit was a 67 in 2007 at the Corona Championship.

OCTOBER 10

"If you put other things ahead of Christ, that's when things get mixed up."

—TURNER WARD, MLB OUTFIELDER

"They gave themselves first of all to the Lord, and then by the will of God also to us."

—2 CORINTHIANS 8:5

Turner Ward enjoyed two World Series championships while playing with the Toronto Blue Jays in 1992 and 1993.

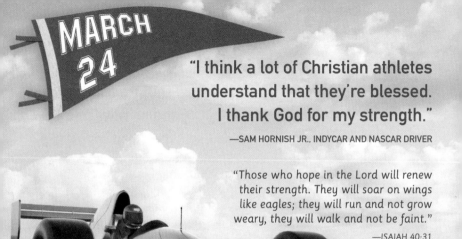

MARCH 24

"I think a lot of Christian athletes understand that they're blessed. I thank God for my strength."

—SAM HORNISH JR., INDYCAR AND NASCAR DRIVER

"Those who hope in the Lord will renew their strength. They will soar on wings like eagles; they will run and not grow weary, they will walk and not be faint."

—ISAIAH 40:31

Sam Hornish Jr. won the 2006 Indianapolis 500, and he was the IndyCar Series champion in three different seasons.

OCTOBER 9

"It gives me great peace to know that no matter how good or how bad I do, the Lord loves me."

—ANDY PETTITTE. MLB ALL-STAR PITCHER

"Therefore, there is now no condemnation for those who are in Christ Jesus."

—ROMANS 8:1

During his long big-league career, Andy Pettitte won 256 games as a left-handed pitcher for the New York Yankees and the Houston Astros, putting him in 42nd position all-time in the majors.

MARCH 25

"It is our choice to keep our eyes and focus on Him and trust Him to take care of the rest."

—JAKE VOSKUHL, NBA CENTER

"We are weak in him, yet by God's power we will live with him to serve you."

—2 CORINTHIANS 13:4

In 1999 Jake Voskuhl was the starting center for the Connecticut Huskies when they won the NCAA championship.

OCTOBER 8

"I want to stay true to what God has called me to do."

—LESLIE FRAZIER,
NFL DEFENSIVE BACK AND HEAD COACH

"Let us not become weary in doing good, for at the proper time we will reap a harvest if we do not give up."

—GALATIANS 6:9

Leslie Frazier, who played for the Chicago Bears in the NFL, became the head coach of the Minnesota Vikings in 2010. After being fired by the Vikings in 2013, he became defensive coordinator for the Tampa Bay Buccaneers.

"Prayer plays a big role in my life."

—GABBY DOUGLAS, OLYMPIC GOLD MEDAL–WINNING GYMNAST

"Rejoice always, pray continually, give
thanks in all circumstances; for this is
God's will for you in Christ Jesus."

—1 THESSALONIANS 5:16–18

In 2012 Gabby Douglas won the individual all-around
gold medal in gymnastics at the Olympic Games.

OCTOBER 7

"Each morning I pray a prayer of surrender to God. I encourage you to make this a daily process."

—BEN UTECHT, NFL TIGHT END

"You were bought at a price. Therefore honor God with your bodies."

—1 CORINTHIANS 6:20

After Ben Utecht's NFL career ended, he recorded a contemporary Christian music album.

MARCH 27

"The plan of salvation is so simple, but so many people miss it because they think they can work their way to heaven."

—R. A. DICKEY, MLB ALL-STAR PITCHER

"Everyone who calls on the name of the Lord will be saved."

—ROMANS 10:13

R. A. Dickey won the Cy Young Award as the best pitcher in the National League in 2012.

OCTOBER 6

"I want to teach young players the Word of God because that will make them better people, better players, better everything."

—MARIANO RIVERA. MLB ALL-STAR PITCHER

"For everything God created is good, and nothing is to be rejected if it is received with thanksgiving, because it is consecrated by the word of God and prayer. If you point these things out to the brothers and sisters, you will be a good minister of Christ Jesus, nourished on the truths of the faith and of the good teaching that you have followed."

—1 TIMOTHY 4:4–6

When Mariano Rivera retired at the end of the 2013 baseball season, he became the last major league baseball player to wear the number 42. MLB retired the number to honor Jackie Robinson, but Rivera was allowed to wear it until he retired.

MARCH 28

"Find your assurance in God;
He is our steady rock."

—AMBER JACOBS,
WNBA GUARD AND COLLEGE HEAD COACH

"For who is God besides the Lord?
And who is the Rock except our God?"

—PSALM 18:31

While playing for Boston College in 2003, Amber Jacobs won back-to-back NCAA tournament games with last-minute shots. Her heroics helped put the Eagles in the Sweet Sixteen.

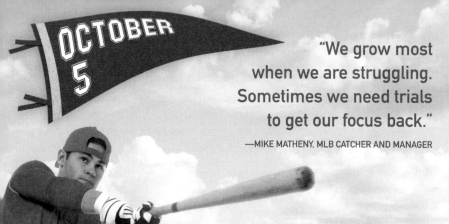

OCTOBER 5

"We grow most when we are struggling. Sometimes we need trials to get our focus back."

—MIKE MATHENY, MLB CATCHER AND MANAGER

"The testing of your faith produces perseverance."

—JAMES 1:3

Mike Matheny spent 13 years in the majors with Milwaukee, Toronto, St. Louis, and San Francisco. In 2011 he was named manager of the St. Louis Cardinals.

"I want to be as clear as water, as open as I can be, for people to understand that no matter who you are, no matter how much you have, if you don't have Jesus Christ as your Savior, it doesn't mean anything."

—MARIANO RIVERA, MLB ALL-STAR PITCHER

"What good is it for someone to gain the whole world, yet forfeit their soul?"

—MARK 8:36

Mariano Rivera recorded 652 saves during his 19-year major league career—the most by any relief pitcher in MLB history.

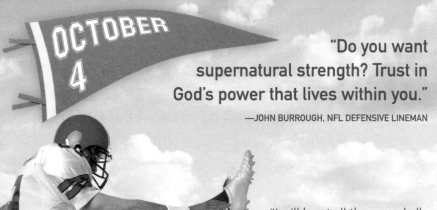

OCTOBER 4

"Do you want supernatural strength? Trust in God's power that lives within you."

—JOHN BURROUGH, NFL DEFENSIVE LINEMAN

"I will boast all the more gladly about my weaknesses, so that God's power may rest on me."

—2 CORINTHIANS 12:9

Before playing in the NFL, John Burrough played college ball for both Washington State and Wyoming.

"God's chastising may seem difficult, but He does not want us to continue in our stagnant lives. Just like a coach, God wants us to be better."

—CAMERON MILLS, NCAA BASKETBALL PLAYER

"I consider that our present sufferings are not worth comparing with the glory that will be revealed in us."

—ROMANS 8:18

During his career at Kentucky, Cameron Mills hit 81 of 171 shots from beyond the arc—a remarkable 47 percent.

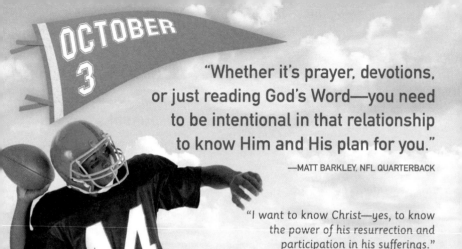

OCTOBER 3

"Whether it's prayer, devotions, or just reading God's Word—you need to be intentional in that relationship to know Him and His plan for you."

—MATT BARKLEY, NFL QUARTERBACK

"I want to know Christ—yes, to know the power of his resurrection and participation in his sufferings."

—PHILIPPIANS 3:10

Matt Barkley played for USC in college and then moved to the NFL in 2013 as the Philadelphia Eagles' backup quarterback in his first season.

"Just as what I eat will affect how I perform on the court, how I fill that void in my soul will affect the peace and joy I experience in my life. What are you hungry for?"

—RUTH RILEY, WNBA ALL-STAR CENTER

"Blessed are those who hunger and thirst for righteousness, for they will be filled."

—MATTHEW 5:6

While playing college basketball at Notre Dame, Ruth Riley scored 2,072 points and led her team to the NCAA championship in 2001.

OCTOBER 2

"I realize that God gave me so many talents, and I want to use them for Him."

—RUSSELL WILSON, NFL QUARTERBACK

"There are different kinds of gifts, but the same Spirit distributes them. There are different kinds of service, but the same Lord. There are different kinds of working, but in all of them and in everyone it is the same God at work."

—1 CORINTHIANS 12:4–6

During his Super Bowl season with the Seattle Seahawks, Russell Wilson was drafted by another team—the Texas Rangers. He had been picked in the MLB draft by the Colorado Rockies, but the Rangers acquired him in December 2013 in a Rule 5 draft.

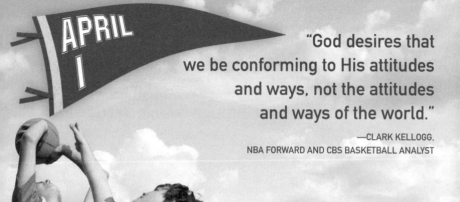

APRIL 1

"God desires that we be conforming to His attitudes and ways, not the attitudes and ways of the world."

—CLARK KELLOGG,
NBA FORWARD AND CBS BASKETBALL ANALYST

"Has not God made foolish the wisdom of the world?"

—1 CORINTHIANS 1:20

Clark Kellogg, who played basketball for Ohio State in college, is a long-time executive for the Indiana Pacers.

OCTOBER
1

"Our perception of self must be grounded in our relationship to God through faith in Jesus Christ."

—FRANK REICH, NFL QUARTERBACK AND COACH

"There is now no condemnation for those who are in Christ Jesus, because through Christ Jesus the law of the Spirit who gives life has set you free from the law of sin and death."

—ROMANS 8:1–2

After retiring from his 13-year NFL career, former quarterback Frank Reich was the president of Reformed Theological Seminary in Charlotte, North Carolina, for three years.

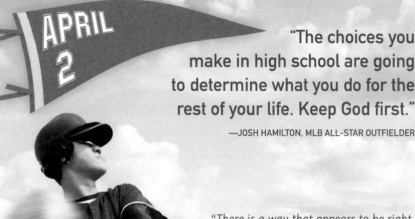

APRIL
2

"The choices you make in high school are going to determine what you do for the rest of your life. Keep God first."

—JOSH HAMILTON, MLB ALL-STAR OUTFIELDER

"There is a way that appears to be right, but in the end it leads to death."

—PROVERBS 14:12

Josh Hamilton was selected as the Most Valuable Player of the American League in 2010.

SEPTEMBER 30

"It's such a great thing to see how God never leaves your side, or is always waiting on you to come back to Him."

—JOSH HAMILTON, MLB ALL-STAR OUTFIELDER

"This is what the Lord says: 'In the time of my favor I will answer you, and in the day of salvation I will help you.'"

—ISAIAH 49:8

In 2008 while playing for the Texas Rangers, Josh Hamilton led the American League in RBI with 130. He also hit 32 home runs and batted .304 that season.

"This generation is hungry for truth and something that is honest, hard-core, sold out. That's how I am able to mesh my two passions—skateboarding and serving the Lord."

—CHRISTIAN HOSOI, PRO SKATEBOARDER

"The heart of the discerning acquires knowledge, for the ears of the wise seek it out."

—PROVERBS 18:15

As a young skateboarder in the 1980s, Christian Hosoi's main competitor was Tony Hawk. Christian marketed a legendary skateboard called the Hammerhead, which has been a bestseller for many years.

SEPTEMBER 29

"My faith helps keep me grounded. I know that no matter what I do here—my success or my failure on the field—that there's a higher thing going on for me with God."

—MARK TEIXEIRA, MLB ALL-STAR FIRST BASEMAN

"I became a servant of this gospel by the gift of God's grace given me through the working of his power."

—EPHESIANS 3:7

In 2009 Mark Teixeira led the American League with 39 home runs and 122 RBI.

APRIL 4

"Our friends are watching—
and our example can lead
them to or away from the Savior."

—JEAN DRISCOLL, CHAMPION WHEELCHAIR MARATHONER

"Whatever you have learned or received or heard
from me, or seen in me—put it into practice.
And the God of peace will be with you."

—PHILIPPIANS 4:9

Jean Driscoll won the Boston Marathon wheelchair
division eight times during her racing career.

SEPTEMBER 28

"While there are many sinful temptations in this profession, it's easy for me to be a witness because I am grounded in my faith and I know where I stand with Christ."

—STEPHEN DREW, MLB SHORTSTOP

"I pray that out of his glorious riches he may strengthen you with power through his Spirit in your inner being, so that Christ may dwell in your hearts through faith. And I pray that you [are] rooted and established in love."

—EPHESIANS 3:16–17

In both 2009 and 2013, Stephen Drew finished second in the league in fielding percentage among shortstops. In 2009 he had a .980 percentage for the Diamondbacks, and in 2013 a .984 percentage for the Red Sox.

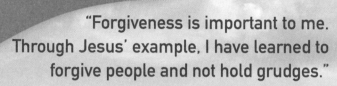

APRIL 5

"Forgiveness is important to me. Through Jesus' example, I have learned to forgive people and not hold grudges."

—EDDIE JOHNSON, MLS STRIKER

"Be kind and compassionate to one another, forgiving each other, just as in Christ God forgave you."

—EPHESIANS 4:32

During a qualifier for the 2014 World Cup of Soccer, Eddie Johnson scored both US goals in a win over Antiqua and Barbuda.

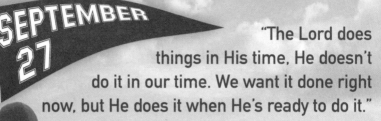

SEPTEMBER 27

"The Lord does things in His time, He doesn't do it in our time. We want it done right now, but He does it when He's ready to do it."

—TED BARRETT, MLB UMPIRE

"There is a time for everything, and a season for every activity under the heavens."

—ECCLESIASTES 3:1

Long-time major league umpire Ted Barrett (he began in 1994) has a PhD in theology from Trinity Theological Seminary.

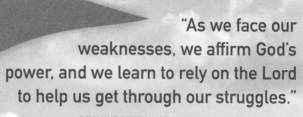

APRIL 6

"As we face our weaknesses, we affirm God's power, and we learn to rely on the Lord to help us get through our struggles."

—ROXANNE ROBBINS, NCAA TRACK, SPORTS JOURNALIST

"That is why, for Christ's sake, I delight in weaknesses, in insults, in hardships, in persecutions, in difficulties. For when I am weak, then I am strong."

—2 CORINTHIANS 12:10

After running for Auburn University, Roxanne enjoyed a career as a sportswriter—attending several Olympic Games. Later she began a ministry in Uganda, where she lives with her son, Wasswa, whom she adopted in Uganda.

SEPTEMBER 26

"When things happen, I ask, 'What would Jesus do in this situation?' When I play ball, it is all for Him."

—JUAN PIERRE, MLB OUTFIELDER

"To this you were called, because Christ suffered for you, leaving you an example, that you should follow in his steps."

—1 PETER 2:21

From 2003 through 2007, Juan Pierre did not miss a game—playing in 162 games each season. In 2004 and 2006, he led the National League in hits (221 and 204).

APRIL 7

"Matthew 5:8 says, 'Blessed are the pure in heart, for they shall see God.' Will you take up the challenge to walk the pure path with me?"

—RYAN HALL, OLYMPIC LONG-DISTANCE RUNNER

"Search me, God, and ... see if there is any offensive way in me."

—PSALM 139:23–24

In 2011 Ryan Hall ran the fastest marathon ever recorded by an American with a 2:04:58 time at the Boston Marathon.

SEPTEMBER 25

"God puts us together, and when we are good at something— we're going to like it. What your passion is, is where God is pushing you to excel."

—MIKE MINTER,
NFL SAFETY AND COLLEGE HEAD COACH

"May he give you the desire of your heart and make all your plans succeed."

—PSALM 20:4

After a 10-year NFL career with the Carolina Panthers, Mike Minter went into coaching. He got his first head coaching position in 2013 as the top man at Campbell University.

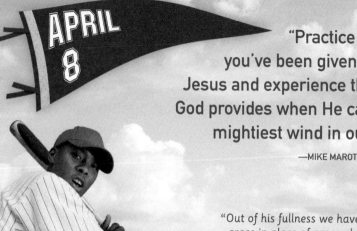

APRIL 8

"Practice the faith you've been given through Jesus and experience the grace God provides when He calms the mightiest wind in our lives."

—MIKE MAROTH, MLB PITCHER

"Out of his fullness we have all received grace in place of grace already given."

—JOHN 1:16

Mike Maroth's pitching career from 2002 through 2007 netted 50 wins for the Detroit Tigers.

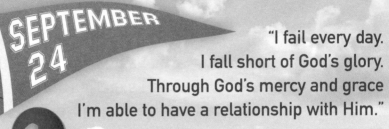

SEPTEMBER 24

"I fail every day.
I fall short of God's glory.
Through God's mercy and grace
I'm able to have a relationship with Him."

—JASON WITTEN, NFL ALL-PRO TIGHT END

"The Word became flesh and
made his dwelling among us.
We have seen his glory, the glory
of the one and only Son, who came
from the Father, full of grace and truth."

—JOHN 1:14

Jason Witten owns Dallas Cowboys records for most career receptions
and most receptions in a game. In 2009 he won the NFL Iron Man Award.

APRIL
9

"In each situation you find yourself, think of how you can use it to help others grow in the Lord."

—DAVID THOMPSON, NBA HALL OF FAME FORWARD

"And who knows but that you have come to your royal position for such a time as this?"

—ESTHER 4:14

Just five players have scored 70 or more points in an NBA game, and David Thompson is one of them. He scored 73 points against Detroit in 1978 while playing for the Denver Nuggets.

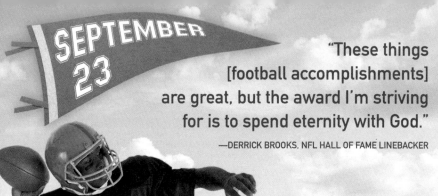

SEPTEMBER 23

"These things [football accomplishments] are great, but the award I'm striving for is to spend eternity with God."

—DERRICK BROOKS, NFL HALL OF FAME LINEBACKER

"Very truly I tell you, whoever hears my word and believes him who sent me has eternal life and will not be judged but has crossed over from death to life."

—JOHN 5:24

Derrick Brooks, who played from 1995 through 2008 for the Tampa Bay Buccaneers, was inducted into the Pro Football Hall of Fame in 2014.

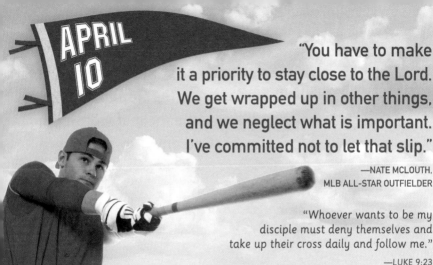

APRIL 10

"You have to make it a priority to stay close to the Lord. We get wrapped up in other things, and we neglect what is important. I've committed not to let that slip."

—NATE MCLOUTH,
MLB ALL-STAR OUTFIELDER

"Whoever wants to be my disciple must deny themselves and take up their cross daily and follow me."

—LUKE 9:23

Nate McLouth was the Pittsburgh Pirates' representative in the 2008 All-Star Game.

"Few will experience the thrill of playing in the Super Bowl, but we can all know the thrill of worshiping God anytime, anywhere."

—MATT STOVER, NFL ALL-PRO KICKER

"Ascribe to the Lord the glory due his name; worship the Lord in the splendor of his holiness."

—PSALM 29:2

In 2000 Matt Stover led the NFL with 35 field goals. He was 35 for 39 for a percentage of 89 percent.

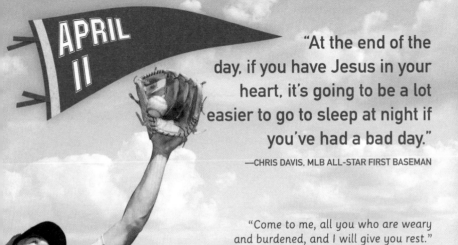

APRIL 11

"At the end of the day, if you have Jesus in your heart, it's going to be a lot easier to go to sleep at night if you've had a bad day."

—CHRIS DAVIS, MLB ALL-STAR FIRST BASEMAN

"Come to me, all you who are weary and burdened, and I will give you rest."

—MATTHEW 11:28

In the first four games of the 2013 season, Chris Davis had four home runs and 16 RBIs—the most RBIs ever in the first four games of a season.

SEPTEMBER 21

"Look ahead to the prize.
Look ahead to Christ!"

—JOHN BURROUGH, NFL DEFENSIVE LINEMAN

"I press on toward the goal to win
the prize for which God has called
me heavenward in Christ Jesus."

—PHILIPPIANS 3:14

John Burrough was drafted by Atlanta in 1995. He spent six full
seasons in the NFL at defense for Atlanta and Minnesota.

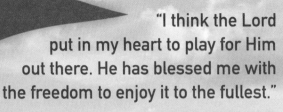

APRIL 12

"I think the Lord put in my heart to play for Him out there. He has blessed me with the freedom to enjoy it to the fullest."

—GAVIN FLOYD, MLB PITCHER

"So I saw that there is nothing better for a person than to enjoy their work, because that is their lot. For who can bring them to see what will happen after them?"

—ECCLESIASTES 3:22

Gavin Floyd's best season as a major league pitcher was 2008 when he went 17–8 for the Chicago White Sox.

SEPTEMBER 20

"Any time I wonder about what I should do, I think, 'How does this affect me? How does this affect God?' I've left a lot of my desires in God's hands, and you can't go wrong when you do that."

—CHRIS DAVIS, MLB ALL-STAR FIRST BASEMAN

"What does the Lord require of you? To act justly and to love mercy and to walk humbly with your God."

—MICAH 6:8

In his first two full seasons playing for the Baltimore Orioles, Chris Davis averaged 43 home runs a year.

APRIL 13

"Friends. Faith.
What a great combination."

—TRACY HANSON, LPGA GOLFER

"Two are better than one, because they have
a good return for their labor: If either of them
falls down, one can help the other up."

—ECCLESIASTES 4:9–10

After a successful golfing career at San Jose State, Tracy Hanson spent a
number of years on the LPGA Tour. Since retiring, she has spent time
writing, traveling, and speaking about her faith.

SEPTEMBER 19

"To grow as a Christian, you need to be in fellowship with God in prayer."

—DON KELLY, MLB INFIELDER/OUTFIELDER

"For the eyes of the Lord are on the righteous and his ears are attentive to their prayer."

—1 PETER 3:12

In the 2011 American League Division Series against the New York Yankees, Don Kelly hit .364 with a home run.

"What do I value the most?
Being on TV? Being a great player?
What the world has to offer? If you seek
God first, not just lip service, your eyes
will open to the glory of God."

—NICK HUNDLEY, MLB CATCHER

"You, God, are my God, earnestly I seek you; I
thirst for you, my whole being longs for you."

—PSALM 63:1

Nick Hundley's dad was defensive coordinator for the University of
Washington from 1999 to 2003. He has also coached at UCLA and UNLV.

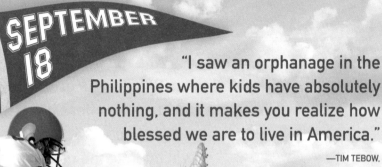

SEPTEMBER 18

"I saw an orphanage in the Philippines where kids have absolutely nothing, and it makes you realize how blessed we are to live in America."

—TIM TEBOW,
NFL QUARTERBACK, ESPN ANALYST

"The generous will themselves be blessed, for they share their food with the poor."

—PROVERBS 22:9

While quarterback for the Florida Gators in college, Tim Tebow set a school record for most rushing touchdowns by a quarterback (57).

APRIL 15

"One of the most rewarding things about training is involving God in the process. Praise God by giving your best and leaning on Him to get through the tough workouts."

—SARA HALL, LONG-DISTANCE RUNNER

"Whatever your hand finds to do, do it with all your might."

—ECCLESIASTES 9:10

Sara Hall and her husband, Ryan, are two of the top long-distance runners in America. They met while attending Stanford.

SEPTEMBER
17

"God alone provides ultimate fulfillment."

—ROXANNE ROBBINS, NCAA TRACK, SPORTS JOURNALIST

"I consider everything a loss because
of the surpassing worth of knowing
Christ Jesus my Lord."

—PHILIPPIANS 3:8

At one time Roxanne Robbins headed up the Heritage Foundation's "Professional
Athletes and At-Risk Youth" initiative, which was used by both the legislative and
executive branches of the US government in making policy regarding young people.

APRIL 16

"The Bible is the key to living life the right way. Use it."

—AARON BADDELEY, PGA GOLFER

"Keep this Book of the Law always on your lips."

—JOSHUA 1:8

As a teenager, Aaron Baddeley won back-to-back Australian Opens.

SEPTEMBER 16

"The awesome thing God does is teach us lessons in adversity."

—CHRISTIAN PONDER, NFL QUARTERBACK

"Do not be surprised at the fiery ordeal that has come on you to test you, as though something strange were happening to you. But rejoice inasmuch as you participate in the sufferings of Christ, so that you may be overjoyed when his glory is revealed."

—1 PETER 4:12–13

Christian Ponder was a quarterback for Florida State while in college. In 2011 he was the MVP of the Senior Bowl. He spent his first three seasons in the NFL with the Minnesota Vikings.

APRIL 17

"If we would learn to let God be in charge, we would have less to worry about in our lives."

—SIEW-AI LIM, LPGA GOLFER

"Commit your way to the Lord; trust in him."

—PSALM 37:5

Siew-Ai Lim's best year on the LPGA Tour was 2004 when she earned over $177,000 in prize money.

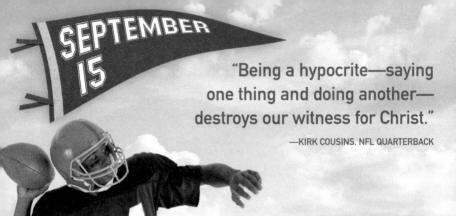

SEPTEMBER 15

"Being a hypocrite—saying one thing and doing another—destroys our witness for Christ."

—KIRK COUSINS, NFL QUARTERBACK

"Rid yourselves of all malice and all deceit, hypocrisy, envy, and slander of every kind."

—1 PETER 2:1

After becoming an NFL player in 2012, Kirk Cousins wrote a book about his faith. It's called *Game Changer*, and it was published by Zonderkidz.

APRIL 18

"By following Jesus' example, we show our love for Him, and we store up treasures in heaven."

—SCOTT MENDES, RODEO RIDER

"If you love me, keep my commands."

—JOHN 14:15

In 1997 Scott Mendes fulfilled a lifelong dream by winning the National Finals Rodeo in Las Vegas—making him the Professional Rodeo Cowboys Association world champion.

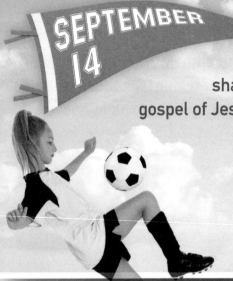

SEPTEMBER 14

"God calls us to
share our faith, to spread the
gospel of Jesus and how He saves us."

—MICHAEL HARRINGTON, MLS DEFENDER

*"The harvest is plentiful but
the workers are few."*

—MATTHEW 9:37

While with Sporting Kansas City in MLS, Michael Harrington
played in 149 regular season games and logged 11,633 minutes of
playing time. In 2013 he started all 33 games for the Portland Timbers.

"You want to represent Christ in a good way on and off the field. You want to be as competitive as you can, but you don't want to lose sight of what's most important, and that's God."

—MICHAEL HARRINGTON, MLS DEFENDER

"You are a chosen people, a royal priesthood, a holy nation, God's special possession, that you may declare the praises of him who called you out of darkness into his wonderful light."

—1 PETER 2:9

In 2007 Michael Harrington finished third in the voting for MLS Rookie of the Year.

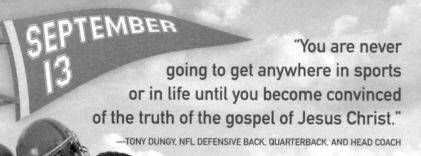

SEPTEMBER 13

"You are never going to get anywhere in sports or in life until you become convinced of the truth of the gospel of Jesus Christ."

—TONY DUNGY, NFL DEFENSIVE BACK, QUARTERBACK, AND HEAD COACH

" 'He himself bore our sins' in his body on the cross, so that we might die to sins and live for righteousness; 'by his wounds you have been healed.' "

—1 PETER 2:24

Best-selling author, Super Bowl–winning coach, and NFL analyst Tony Dungy has become one of the most respected men in America—in sports and out.

APRIL 20

"Until you accept Christ into your life, you will never be fully fulfilled."

—JEFF FRANCOEUR, MLB OUTFIELDER

"Open their eyes and turn them from darkness to light, and from the power of Satan to God, so that they may receive forgiveness of sins and a place among those who are sanctified by faith in me."

—ACTS 26:18

In 2007 Jeff Francoeur was presented with the Gold Glove Award, which honored him for being one of the best fielders in baseball.

"As a Christian, our first priority should be a willingness to give up any liberty we have so we can lead someone to Christ."

—GILL BYRD, NFL CORNERBACK/SAFETY

"In your relationships with one another, have the same mindset as Christ Jesus."

—PHILIPPIANS 2:5

Gill Byrd enjoyed two Pro Bowl seasons at cornerback for the San Diego Chargers (1991 and 1992). His son Jairus earned Pro Bowl honors as a free safety in 2009.

APRIL 21

"My concern before my fellow players is to never say one thing and be something else. I seek to be a role model."

—KAKÁ, BRAZILIAN SOCCER MIDFIELDER

"Anyone who claims to be in the light but hates a brother or sister is still in the darkness."

—1 JOHN 2:9

In 2007 Kaká was named the World Player of the Year in soccer.

SEPTEMBER
11

"Since you woke up this morning, have you been feeding the flesh or the Spirit?"

—RON BROWN, NCAA FOOTBALL COACH

"The fruit of the Spirit is love."

—GALATIANS 5:22

A long-time assistant coach at Nebraska, Ron Brown has been both running backs coach and tight ends coach. Many of his players have moved on the next level and have played in the NFL.

APRIL 22

"What I want to do now is stay humble and grow in the Word."

—JONATHAN BYRD, PGA GOLFER

"For those who exalt themselves will be humbled, and those who humble themselves will be exalted."

—MATTHEW 23:12

From 2002 through 2011 Jonathan Byrd won five PGA tournaments: the Buick Challenge, the B.C. Open, the John Deere Classic, the Shriners Hospitals for Children Open, and the Hyundai Tournament of Champions.

SEPTEMBER 10

"God can give us strength and protection as we seek to be good examples for those who are watching us."

—BRANDON WEBB, MLB ALL-STAR PITCHER

"My life is an example to many, because you have been my strength and protection."

—PSALM 71:7 (NEW LIVING TRANSLATION)

Ashland, Kentucky, native Brandon Webb led the National League in shutouts in both 2006 and 2007 with three in each of those seasons. He finished his injury-shortened career with eight shutouts.

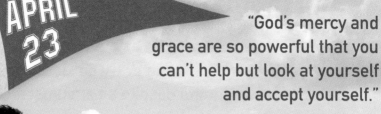

APRIL 23

"God's mercy and grace are so powerful that you can't help but look at yourself and accept yourself."

—TIM HOWARD, SOCCER GOALIE

"Because of his great love for us, God, who is rich in mercy, made us alive with Christ."

—EPHESIANS 2:4–5

In his first World Cup game as goalkeeper for the US in the 2010 tournament against England, Tim Howard was named Man of the Match.

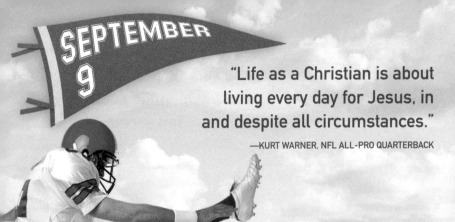

SEPTEMBER 9

"Life as a Christian is about living every day for Jesus, in and despite all circumstances."

—KURT WARNER, NFL ALL-PRO QUARTERBACK

"Give thanks in all circumstances; for this is God's will for you in Christ Jesus."

—1 THESSALONIANS 5:18

Kurt Warner was selected MVP of the National Football League in both 2001 and 2008.

"From time to time in my life, I've had a little trouble feeling accepted by others. That can happen when you end up being seven feet tall. But I've found someone who always accepts me and cares for me. His name is Jesus Christ."

—DAVID ROBINSON, NBA HALL OF FAME CENTER

"It is for freedom that Christ has set us free. Stand firm, then."

—GALATIANS 5:1

Toward the end of his playing career in the NBA, David Robinson founded the Carver Academy, a school in San Antonio, to provide more opportunities for inner-city kids.

SEPTEMBER 8

"I try to represent Christ in everything I do."

—DAN ALEXANDER, NFL FULLBACK

"We are therefore Christ's ambassadors, as though God were making his appeal through us."

—2 CORINTHIANS 5:20

After a successful college career at Nebraska, Dan Alexander spent three years in the NFL with Tennessee, Jacksonville, and St. Louis. Later he played for a few years in the Arena Football League.

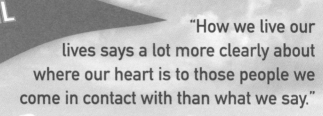

APRIL 25

"How we live our lives says a lot more clearly about where our heart is to those people we come in contact with than what we say."

—LANCE BERKMAN, MLB ALL-STAR FIRST BASEMAN

"Therefore, as we have opportunity, let us do good to all people, especially to those who belong to the family of believers."

—GALATIANS 6:10

During his major league career, Lance Berkman hit 422 doubles (145th of all-time). Twice he led the National League in doubles (55 in 2001 and 46 in 2008).

"Whether in the middle of competition or doing things calmly at home, make a point to think about excellent and praiseworthy things."

—JEAN DRISCOLL, WHEELCHAIR MARATHON CHAMPION

"Finally, brothers and sisters, whatever is true, whatever is noble, whatever is right, whatever is pure, whatever is lovely, whatever is admirable—if anything is excellent or praiseworthy—think about such things."

—PHILIPPIANS 4:8

Jean Driscoll won 12 medals in the Summer Paralympic Games—five gold, three silver, and four bronze. She competed in 1988, 1992, 1996, and 2000.

APRIL 26

"God knows what your need is right now. Talk to Him about it."

—KRISTEN SAMP, LPGA GOLFER

"Therefore I tell you, do not worry about your life."

—MATTHEW 6:25

After Kristen Samp graduated from the University of Missouri in 1996, she joined the Futures Tour, where she displayed her spiritual maturity by heading up the Fellowship of Christian Athletes Golf Fellowship for two seasons.

SEPTEMBER 6

"I have the Holy Spirit in me, which is the power of God to help me go the extra mile."

—STEFEN WISNIEWSKI, NFL OFFENSIVE LINEMAN

"May the God of hope fill you with all joy and peace as you trust in him, so that you may overflow with hope by the power of the Holy Spirit."

—ROMANS 15:13

The son of a former NFL player, Leo Wisniewski, Stefen was drafted in 2011 by the Oakland Raiders after an academic All-American career at Penn State.

APRIL 27

"If we trust in God
and seek His kingdom first,
His righteousness
can be ours."

—RUSS ORTIZ, MLB ALL-STAR PITCHER

"But seek first [God's] kingdom
and his righteousness, and all these
things will be given to you as well."

—MATTHEW 6:33

In 2003 Russ Ortiz led the National League with 21 victories and was an All-Star.
His team, the Atlanta Braves, made the playoffs, and he even hit two home runs.

SEPTEMBER 5

"If there are opportunities to show Christ as a player, I'm more excited to do that than anything else."

—GAVIN FLOYD, MLB PITCHER

"You will receive power when the Holy Spirit comes on you; and you will be my witnesses in Jerusalem, and in all Judea and Samaria, and to the ends of the earth."

—ACTS 1:8

Gavin Floyd's strength as a pitcher is his variety of pitches: a four-seam fastball, a two-seam fastball, a slider, a curve, and a changeup.

APRIL 28

"By developing a relationship with God through prayer, we can have the confidence that He is always there."

—PAUL GRAFER, MLS GOALIE

"This is what the Lord says, ... 'You will seek me and find me when you seek me with all your heart.'"

—JEREMIAH 29:10, 13

In the MLS, Paul Grafer played for the Colorado Rapids and the MetroStars.

SEPTEMBER 4

"When we neglect the preparation of our lives spiritually, we set ourselves up for failure."

—KIRK COUSINS, NFL QUARTERBACK

"Put on the full armor of God, so that you can take your stand against the devil's schemes."

—EPHESIANS 6:11

After a successful prep career, Kirk Cousins moved on to Michigan State. He was drafted by the Washington Redskins in the same draft as Robert Griffin III.

APRIL 29

"A lot of kids watch everything we do. So you just try to live your life as best you can in a way that reflects Christ's image."

—BRIAN ROBERTS, MLB ALL-STAR INFIELDER

"Follow my example, as I follow the example of Christ."

—1 CORINTHIANS 11:1

Brian Roberts did something only three other players have done: He hit 50 doubles in a season three times. The other three? Hall of Famers Tris Speaker, Paul Waner, and Stan Musial.

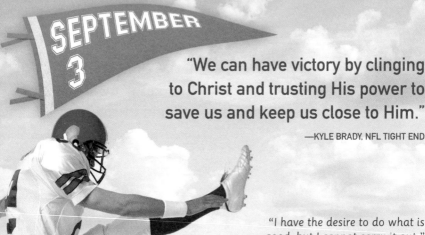

SEPTEMBER 3

"We can have victory by clinging to Christ and trusting His power to save us and keep us close to Him."

—KYLE BRADY, NFL TIGHT END

"I have the desire to do what is good, but I cannot carry it out."

—ROMANS 7:18

Kyle Brady played tight end for the Jets, the Jacksonville Jaguars, and the New England Patriots during his 13-year NFL career. Brady started at tight end for the Patriots in Super Bowl XLII.

APRIL 30

"It's taken a lot of pressure off me knowing that God is in charge of my life, no matter where He sends me."

—JOE GIRARDI, MLB ALL-STAR CATCHER AND MANAGER

"In his hand is the life of every creature and the breath of all mankind."

—JOB 12:10

Joe Girardi was named the National League Manager of the Year in 2006 as the skipper of the Florida Marlins.

SEPTEMBER 2

"Trusting God is not easy. But by developing a relationship with Him through prayer, we can have confidence that He is always there."

—PAUL GRAFER, MLS GOALIE

"For everyone who asks receives; the one who seeks finds; and to the one who knocks, the door will be opened."

—LUKE 11:10

After his MLS playing career was over, Paul Grafer became the director of SAFE, an organization that helps student-athletes manage their lives financially.

MAY 1

"Win or lose, God can use any of us to glorify Him. The next generation of Christians needs to know how much God loves them."

—JOSH DAVIS, OLYMPIC GOLD MEDAL–WINNING SWIMMER

"May I never boast except in the cross of our Lord Jesus Christ, through which the world has been crucified to me, and I to the world."

—GALATIANS 6:14

During his swimming career, Josh Davis earned over a dozen medals in international swimming competitions.

SEPTEMBER 1

"As a Christian, you want to give glory and honor to the Lord."

—ADRIAN GONZALEZ, MLB ALL-STAR FIRST BASEMAN

"Not to us, Lord, not to us but to your name be the glory, because of your love and faithfulness."

—PSALM 115:1

In 2011 Adrian Gonzalez led the American League in hits with 213. He hit .338 that season for Boston.

MAY
2

"No one cares what we say if our actions do not match our words."

—KYLE ABBOTT, MLB PITCHER

"Dear children, let us not love with words or speech but with actions and in truth."

—1 JOHN 3:18

Kyle Abbott found his most success as a reliever with the Phillies in 1995, going 2–0 with an ERA of 3.81. He later operated Pro Source Athletics in Carrollton, Texas.

AUGUST 31

"God has a plan for
each person. I am thankful
that I can trust each day to Him."

—LEAH O'BRIEN-AMICO,
OLYMPIC GOLD MEDAL–WINNING SOFTBALL PLAYER

*"All the days ordained for me were written in
your book before one of them came to be."*

—PSALM 139:16

Leah O'Brien-Amico was named to the Athletes in Action Hall of Faith in 2008.

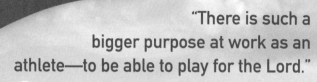

MAY 3

"There is such a bigger purpose at work as an athlete—to be able to play for the Lord."

—GAVIN FLOYD, MLB PITCHER

"That is why we labor and strive, because we have put our hope in the living God."

—1 TIMOTHY 4:10

From 2008 through 2012, Gavin Floyd won at least 10 games a season for the Chicago White Sox. He spent his first season with the Atlanta Braves in 2014.

AUGUST 30

"We need to listen for God's voice through reading the Bible, and then do what He tells us."

—MATT DIAZ, MLB OUTFIELDER

"Show me your ways, Lord; teach me your paths. Guide me in your truth and teach me."

—PSALM 25:4–5

For his efforts as a college baseball player, Matt Diaz was named the *Sporting News* Man of the Year in 1998.

MAY 4

"With Christ in my life, soccer's been put into perspective. There are those days you don't feel like practicing, but you do it because you're playing for Christ in everything you do."

—MIKE CLARK, MLS DEFENDER

"Whatever you do, whether in word or deed, do it all in the name of the Lord Jesus, giving thanks to God the Father through him."

—COLOSSIANS 3:17

After graduating from Indiana University, Mike Clark joined the Columbus Crew as a part of the first MLS draft. By the time he retired from the Crew in 2004, he held team records in games played, minutes played, and games started.

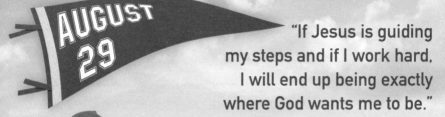

AUGUST 29

"If Jesus is guiding my steps and if I work hard, I will end up being exactly where God wants me to be."

—JEREMY AFFELDT, MLB PITCHER

"In their hearts humans plans their course, but the Lord establishes their steps."

—PROVERBS 16:9

In 2009 Jeremy Affeldt fashioned a 1.73 ERA for San Francisco and was named the winner of the This Year in Baseball Setup Man of the Year Award.

"We reach out to our teammates, friends, and the people God has put in our life— even when it is inconvenient for us. When we do this, we will discover the satisfying joy that only comes through serving others."

—SARA HALL, LONG-DISTANCE RUNNER

"And whoever wants to be first must be slave of all. For even the Son of Man did not come to be served, but to serve, and to give his life as a ransom for many."

—MARK 10:44–45

Running stars Sara and Ryan Hall have established the Hall Steps Foundation, which is dedicated to fighting global poverty through better health practices.

"I have found that
the best way to be successful is
to think as the apostle John suggested,
'[Christ] must increase, but I must decrease.'"

—MICHAEL BARRETT, MLB CATCHER

"[Jesus] must become greater;
I must become less."

—JOHN 3:30

While playing for the Chicago Cubs from 2004 through 2006,
Michael Barrett hit 16 home runs in all three of those seasons.

MAY 6

"People are going to make mistakes and fall down. It's up to us as Christians to pick them up."

—CHRIS DAVIS, MLB ALL-STAR FIRST BASEMAN

"In humility value others above yourselves, not looking to your own interests but each of you to the interests of the others."

—PHILIPPIANS 2:3–4

On May 6, 2012, Chris Davis went 0-for-8 at the plate in a 17-inning game between Baltimore and Boston. But he ended up being the winning pitcher in that game when Buck Showalter ran out of pitchers and let first baseman Davis pitch the 16th inning. The O's won in the 17th inning.

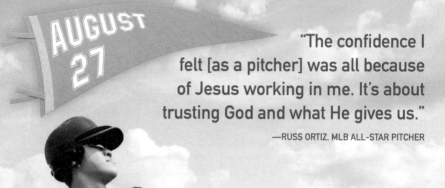

AUGUST 27

"The confidence I felt [as a pitcher] was all because of Jesus working in me. It's about trusting God and what He gives us."

—RUSS ORTIZ, MLB ALL-STAR PITCHER

"The Spirit God gave us does not make us timid, but gives us power, love and self-discipline."

—2 TIMOTHY 1:7

In addition to his pitching prowess, Russ Ortiz was a pretty good hitter. He hit six career home runs and 22 doubles as a major leaguer.

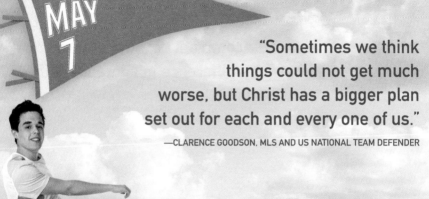

MAY 7

"Sometimes we think things could not get much worse, but Christ has a bigger plan set out for each and every one of us."

—CLARENCE GOODSON, MLS AND US NATIONAL TEAM DEFENDER

"I know that you can do all things; no purpose of yours can be thwarted."

—JOB 42:2

While playing for the US National Team, Clarence Goodson scored five goals in international competition from 2009 through 2013.

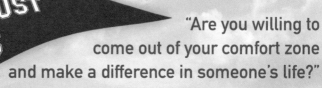

AUGUST 26

"Are you willing to come out of your comfort zone and make a difference in someone's life?"

—LAVONNA MARTIN-FLOREAL,
OLYMPIC SILVER MEDAL–WINNING SPRINTER

"Dear friends, since God so loved us, we also ought to love one another."

—1 JOHN 4:11

LaVonna Martin won the silver medal in the 1992 Olympic Games for the United States in the 100 meter hurdles. LaVonna's husband, Edrick Floreal, is a college track coach (Stanford and Kentucky). Their son EJ played basketball for the Wildcats.

"I've been through some miserable times in baseball, but there are lots worse things in this life. I finally realized that God was in control, and I can look back and see how much God has taken care of me."

—NICK HUNDLEY, MLB CATCHER

"The Lord himself goes before you and will be with you; he will never leave you nor forsake you. Do not be afraid; do not be discouraged."

—DEUTERONOMY 31:8

When he was 12 years old, future major league catcher Nick Hundley played on a youth baseball team that also included James Shields and Ryan Braun.

AUGUST
25

"The Bible is where
the answers are."

—CHAD MOELLER, MLB CATCHER

"Jesus answered, 'It is written: "Man shall
not live on bread alone, but on every word
that comes from the mouth of God." ' "

—MATTHEW 4:4

Chad Moeller spent 10 years in the major leagues. In his best season
Moeller, a catcher, hit .286 for the Arizona Diamondbacks.

"What Jesus did on that cross saved me and freed me from my struggles. I have learned by faith that He has cleansed my heart."

—PAUL BYRD, MLB ALL-STAR PITCHER

"You were washed, you were sanctified, you were justified in the name of the Lord Jesus Christ and by the Spirit of our God."

—1 CORINTHIANS 6:11

Paul Byrd pitched in the major leagues for the Mets, Braves, Phillies, Royals, Angels, Indians, and Red Sox—winning 109 games, including 17 wins for Kansas City in 2002.

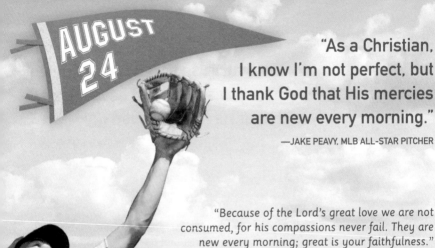

AUGUST
24

"As a Christian,
I know I'm not perfect, but
I thank God that His mercies
are new every morning."

—JAKE PEAVY, MLB ALL-STAR PITCHER

*"Because of the Lord's great love we are not
consumed, for his compassions never fail. They are
new every morning; great is your faithfulness."*

—LAMENTATIONS 3:22–23

Jake Peavy was named to three All-Star teams as a major league pitcher.

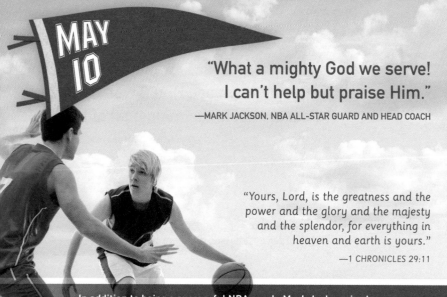

MAY
10

"What a mighty God we serve!
I can't help but praise Him."

—MARK JACKSON, NBA ALL-STAR GUARD AND HEAD COACH

"Yours, Lord, is the greatness and the
power and the glory and the majesty
and the splendor, for everything in
heaven and earth is yours."

—1 CHRONICLES 29:11

In addition to being a successful NBA coach, Mark Jackson is also
an ordained minister and pastor of a church in Van Nuys, California.

"I want to be like Him. I want to please Him. I want to be like Jesus. That is the main goal of my life."

—SHANE HAMMAN, OLYMPIC WEIGHTLIFTER

"For it is God who works in you to will and to act in order to fulfill his good purpose."

—PHILIPPIANS 2:13

Shane Hamman won the gold medal in the +105 kg category in weightlifting in the Pan American Games in 1999. He competed in both the 2000 and 2004 Summer Olympics in weightlifting.

"Nobody else can be like Jesus, and that's why He forgives us. I want to try to be like Him, while at the same time knowing that you can't be like Him."

—ALBERT PUJOLS, MLB ALL-STAR FIRST BASEMAN

"In him we have redemption through his blood, the forgiveness of sins, in accordance with the riches of God's grace."

—EPHESIANS 1:7

Albert Pujols was the National League Rookie of the Year in 2001. In 2014 he reached the 500-home run mark, a level only 26 major league players have ever reached.

AUGUST 22

"I do what I need to do to stay focused on Him, and in return, He blesses me. Our focus needs to be on Him, because we can't do it on our own."

—BRYAN CLAY, OLYMPIC GOLD MEDAL–WINNING DECATHLETE

"[Let us fix] our eyes on Jesus, the pioneer and perfecter of faith."

—HEBREWS 12:2

Bryan Clay earned the label "World's Greatest Athlete" in 2008 when he won decathlon gold at the Beijing Olympic Games.

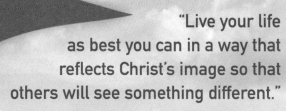

MAY 12

"Live your life as best you can in a way that reflects Christ's image so that others will see something different."

—BRIAN ROBERTS, MLB ALL-STAR SECOND BASEMAN

"Let your light shine before others, that they may see your good deeds and glorify your Father in heaven."

—MATTHEW 5:16

Brian Roberts began his major league career in 2001 as a Baltimore Oriole. His best year was 2005 when he hit .315 for the O's. He joined the New York Yankees in 2014.

AUGUST 21

"Even if you have a rough day, keep trusting the Lord. He has a fantastic reward waiting for you in heaven."

—LEAH O'BRIEN-AMICO,
OLYMPIC GOLD MEDAL–WINNING SOFTBALL PLAYER

"We ... glory in our sufferings, because we know that suffering produces perseverance."

—ROMANS 5:3

Leah O'Brien was a three-time Olympic gold medalist in softball for the United States (1996, 2000, and 2004).

MAY 13

"I believe and understand that God is in control of everything."

—MARIANO RIVERA, MLB ALL-STAR PITCHER

"The Lord works out everything to its proper end."

—PROVERBS 16:4

Mariano Rivera's 652 saves propelled him 51 saves past the next person on the list: Trevor Hoffman.

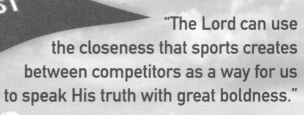

AUGUST 20

"The Lord can use the closeness that sports creates between competitors as a way for us to speak His truth with great boldness."

—BARB LINDQUIST, OLYMPIC TRIATHLETE

"Let your conversation be always full of grace, seasoned with salt, so that you may know how to answer everyone."

—COLOSSIANS 4:6

In 2003 Barb Lindquist was the No. 1 ranked women's triathlete in the world.

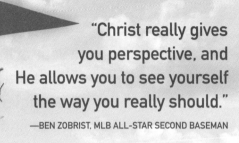

MAY 14

"Christ really gives you perspective, and He allows you to see yourself the way you really should."

—BEN ZOBRIST, MLB ALL-STAR SECOND BASEMAN

"You, therefore, have no excuse, you who pass judgment on someone else, for at whatever point you judge another, you are condemning yourself, because you who pass judgment do the same things."

—ROMANS 2:1

In one game in 2011, Ben Zobrist picked up eight runs batted in, a Tampa Bay Rays record. The Rays beat Minnesota 15–3 in the game.

AUGUST 19

"You have a plan for your own life, and God says, 'This is my plan, and it's better than yours.' I struggled one year, and God said, 'You need to find out who I say you are.' "

—NICK HUNDLEY, MLB CATCHER

"As for God, his way is perfect: The Lord's word is flawless; he shields all who take refuge in him."

—PSALM 18:30

In 2012 Nick Hundley of the San Diego Padres won the Heart & Hustle Award for the Padres. It is given to a player who "demonstrates a passion for the game of baseball and best embodies the values, spirit, and traditions of the game."

"How you choose your friends will have a huge effect on whether your dreams will become a reality. God has a will for you, but it's up to you (with the Holy Spirit's help) to achieve it."

—JEREMY AFFELDT, MLB PITCHER

"You guide me with your counsel."

—PSALM 73:24

Jeremy Affeldt compiled an ERA of 0.00 in the 2012 World Series for the San Francisco Giants.

AUGUST 18

"Take some time to figure out what adjustments you need to make in your life to put God first, and then ask God to help you make them."

—BETHANY HAMILTON DIRKS, PROFESSIONAL SURFER

"I have been crucified with Christ and I no longer live, but Christ lives in me. The life I now live in the body, I live by faith in the Son of God, who loved me and gave himself for me."

—GALATIANS 2:20

Bethany Hamilton and Adam Dirks, who works with the Christian organization Young Life, were married in August 2013. Bethany continues to surf and do some acting.

"If you make good decisions every day along the way, good things have a better chance of happening later."

—BRANDON WEBB, MLB ALL-STAR PITCHER

"Whatever you do, work at it with all your heart, as working for the Lord, not for human masters."

—COLOSSIANS 3:23

Brandon Webb won the Cy Young Award in the National League in 2006.

AUGUST 17

"God was never shy about me.
Why should I be shy about Him?
So I'm not shy about the gospel."

—MARIANO RIVERA, MLB ALL-STAR PITCHER

"For I am not ashamed of the gospel,
because it is the power of God that brings
salvation to everyone who believes: first
to the Jew, then to the Gentile."

—ROMANS 1:16

When Mariano Rivera signed with the New York Yankees as a
20-year-old from the Dominican Republic, he received $3,000.
His last contract with the Yankees in 2013 paid him $10 million.

"Knowing Christ and walking with Him each day—reading the Bible and praying—these give life meaning and allow us to live with joy, not regret."

—MICHAEL BARRETT, MLB CATCHER

"Believe in the Lord Jesus, and you will be saved."

—ACTS 16:31

In 2006 Michael Barrett had his best season, hitting .307 with the Chicago Cubs and pounding out 16 home runs.

AUGUST 16

"Let's go out and give God our best."

—MATT DIAZ, MLB OUTFIELDER

"Lazy hands make for poverty,
but diligent hands bring wealth."

—PROVERBS 10:4

During his 11-year major league career, Matt Diaz banged out 546 hits in 736 games. He hit over .300 three times in his career. His brother, Jonny Diaz, is a contemporary Christian music recording artist.

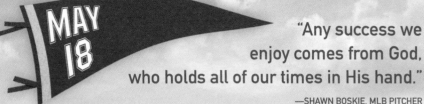

MAY 18

"Any success we enjoy comes from God, who holds all of our times in His hand."

—SHAWN BOSKIE, MLB PITCHER

"But I trust in you, Lord;
I say, 'You are my God.'
My times are in your hands."

—PSALM 31:14-15

A first-round pick of the Chicago Cubs in 1986, Shawn Boskie pitched for six different teams. Boskie's best year was 1996 when he won 12 games for the Angels.

AUGUST 15

"Loving God equals seeking God— which leads to knowing God."

—KATHERINE HULL, LPGA GOLFER

"Come near to God and he will come near to you."

—JAMES 4:8

One of Katherine Hull's best years on the LPGA circuit was 2005 when she won more than $200,000—helped along by finishing second at the BMO Financial Group Canadian Women's Open.

MAY 19

"We are all working toward a common goal—to let others know the great love Christ has to offer us."

—WENDY WARD, LPGA GOLFER

"Go into all the world and preach the gospel to all creation."

—MARK 16:15

During her career on the LPGA Tour, golfer Wendy Ward won four tournaments and nearly $5 million in prize money.

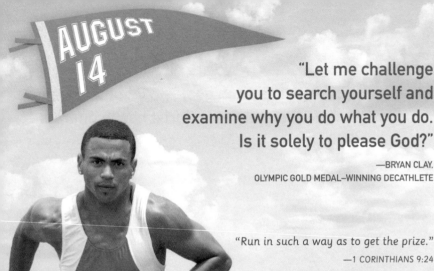

AUGUST
14

"Let me challenge
you to search yourself and
examine why you do what you do.
Is it solely to please God?"

—BRYAN CLAY,
OLYMPIC GOLD MEDAL–WINNING DECATHLETE

"Run in such a way as to get the prize."

—1 CORINTHIANS 9:24

Bryan Clay was featured on a Wheaties cereal box
after his 2008 gold-medal Olympic showing.

MAY 20

"God is calling us to see past today and to focus on things that are eternal."

—MATT DIAZ, MLB OUTFIELDER

"Store up for yourselves treasures in heaven ... For where your treasure is, there your heart will be also."

—MATTHEW 6:20–21

Matt Diaz's best season in the majors was 2007 when he hit .338 for the Atlanta Braves.

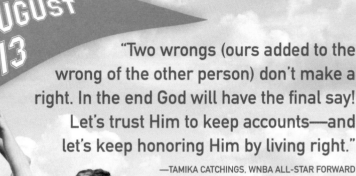

AUGUST 13

"Two wrongs (ours added to the wrong of the other person) don't make a right. In the end God will have the final say! Let's trust Him to keep accounts—and let's keep honoring Him by living right."

—TAMIKA CATCHINGS, WNBA ALL-STAR FORWARD

"Do not take revenge, my dear friends, but leave room for God's wrath."

—ROMANS 12:19

Tamika Catchings has earned three Olympic gold medals as a member of the US Olympic championship team in 2004, 2008, and 2012.

"When fear or doubt creeps into our thoughts, we need to do what God commanded Joshua to do: Be strong and courageous!"

—SCOTT FLETCHER, MLB INFIELDER

"Be strong and courageous."

—DEUTERONOMY 31:6

After being a first-round draft pick in 1979, Fletcher went on to accumulate 1,376 hits during his 15-year career with the Cubs, White Sox, Rangers, Brewers, Red Sox, and Tigers.

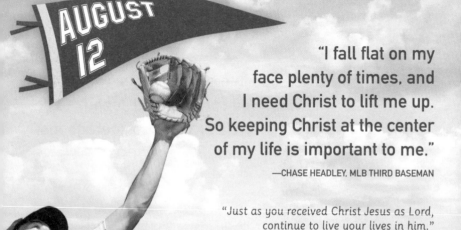

AUGUST 12

"I fall flat on my face plenty of times, and I need Christ to lift me up. So keeping Christ at the center of my life is important to me."

—CHASE HEADLEY, MLB THIRD BASEMAN

"Just as you received Christ Jesus as Lord, continue to live your lives in him."

—COLOSSIANS 2:6

In 2012 Chase Headley finished fifth in voting for the Most Valuable Player Award in the National League. He hit 31 home runs and knocked in 115 runs that season for the San Diego Padres.

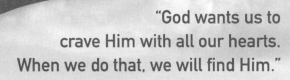

MAY 22

"God wants us to crave Him with all our hearts. When we do that, we will find Him."

—JEREMY AFFELDT, MLB PITCHER

" 'For I know the plans I have for you,' declares the Lord."

—JEREMIAH 29:11

As he entered the 2014 season, Jeremy Affeldt was tenth among active pitchers with 660 appearances—42 as a starter and the rest in relief.

AUGUST 11

"The constant thing I've learned in my life with Christ is perseverance. It's a constant battle of knowing about my special bond with Christ."

—CAT REDDICK WHITEHILL, OLYMPIC GOLD MEDAL–WINNING SOCCER PLAYER

"Blessed is the one who perseveres under trial because, having stood the test, that person will receive the crown of life that the Lord has promised to those who love him."

—JAMES 1:12

"You need to persevere so that when you have done the will of God, you will receive what he has promised."

—HEBREWS 10:36

Cat Reddick was a member of the 2004 US gold medal team in the Olympics. She also played in the World Cup in 2003 and 2007. In the 2007 World Cup, she played in every minute of all six of the United States' games.

MAY 23

"We are called to love people not because they love us but because God loved us."

—JENNY BOUCEK, WNBA PLAYER AND COACH

"Let us love one another, for love comes from God. Everyone who loves has been born of God and knows God."

—1 JOHN 4:7

Jenny Boucek played collegiately at the University of Virginia, after which she joined the Cleveland Rockers for their first season in 1997. She has coached in the WNBA for Washington, Miami, Seattle, and Sacramento.

AUGUST 10

"We can worry ourselves sick—
and worry is such a sin!
Just give your worries to God."

—MARY LOU RETTON KELLEY,
OLYMPIC GOLD MEDAL–WINNING GYMNAST

"Peace I leave with you; my peace I give you.
I do not give to you as the world gives. Do not let
your hearts be troubled and do not be afraid."

—JOHN 14:27

In 1984 Mary Lou Retton was perhaps the most famous athlete in America. She captured the national heart with her gold-medal winning All-Around performance at the Los Angeles Olympic Games by scoring a perfect 10 on the vault. She and her husband, Shannon, have four daughters.

MAY 24

"Baseball is just a game. It's not so much how you play, but how you represent God while you're playing."

—CLAYTON KERSHAW, MLB ALL-STAR PITCHER

"Join together in following my example, brothers and sisters, and just as you have us as a model, keep your eyes on those who live as we do."

—PHILIPPIANS 3:17

Clayton Kershaw was named the Cy Young Award winner in the National League in 2011 and 2013.

"God has blessed me, and if my pitching in the World Series can somehow tell a kid somewhere that it is cool to love Jesus—that would be awesome."

—ADAM WAINWRIGHT, MLB ALL-STAR PITCHER

"I have become all things to all people so that by all possible means I might save some. I do all this for the sake of the gospel, that I may share in its blessings."

—1 CORINTHIANS 9:22–23

Pitcher Adam Wainwright helped the St. Louis Cardinals capture a World Series title in 2006. In 2009 Wainwright led the National League in wins with 19; in 2010 he won 20 games for the Cards.

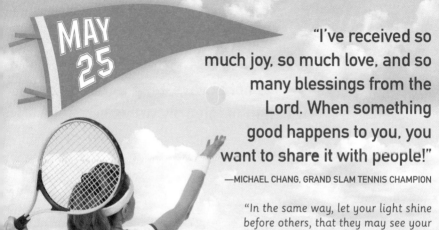

MAY 25

"I've received so much joy, so much love, and so many blessings from the Lord. When something good happens to you, you want to share it with people!"

—MICHAEL CHANG, GRAND SLAM TENNIS CHAMPION

"In the same way, let your light shine before others, that they may see your good deeds and glorify your Father in heaven."

—MATTHEW 5:16

Michael Chang became the youngest male tennis player to win a Grand Slam when he captured the French Open in 1989 at age 17.

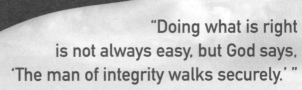

AUGUST
8

"Doing what is right is not always easy, but God says, 'The man of integrity walks securely.'"

—TRACY HANSON, LPGA GOLFER

"May integrity and uprightness protect me, because my hope, Lord, is in you."

—PSALM 25:21

In 2014 former LPGA golfer Tracy Hanson attended the Winter Olympic Games as a part of a group of international sports chaplains.

MAY 26

"I try to be as godly as I can around my teammates, because I know they are always watching. When the opportunity is right, I talk to them about Christianity."

—STEPHEN DREW, MLB SHORTSTOP

"Encourage the young men to be self-controlled. In everything set them an example by doing what is good."

—TITUS 2:6–7

The third Drew brother to play in the majors, Stephen has played for Oakland and Boston since he broke into the league with the Diamondbacks in 2012.

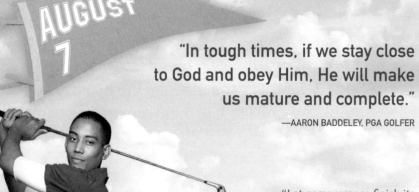

AUGUST 7

"In tough times, if we stay close to God and obey Him, He will make us mature and complete."

—AARON BADDELEY, PGA GOLFER

"Let perseverance finish its work so that you may be mature and complete."

—JAMES 1:4

Aaron Baddeley has long been considered one of the best putters on the PGA tour.

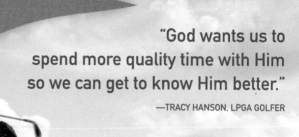

MAY 27

"God wants us to spend more quality time with Him so we can get to know Him better."

—TRACY HANSON, LPGA GOLFER

"Your face, Lord, I will seek."

—PSALM 27:8

After a successful golfing career at San Jose State, Tracy Hanson spent a number of years on the LPGA Tour. Since retiring, she has spent time writing, traveling, and speaking about her faith.

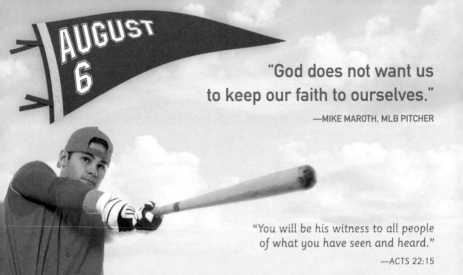

AUGUST
6

"God does not want us
to keep our faith to ourselves."

—MIKE MAROTH, MLB PITCHER

"You will be his witness to all people
of what you have seen and heard."

—ACTS 22:15

Mike Maroth and his wife, Brooke, received the 2004 Bill Emerson
Good Samaritan Award for their philanthropic work through a group
called Rock and Wrap It Up, which distributes food to the needy.

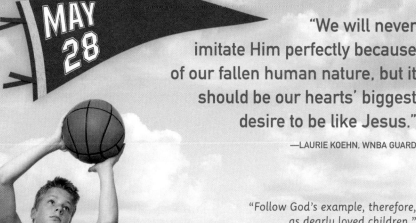

MAY 28

"We will never imitate Him perfectly because of our fallen human nature, but it should be our hearts' biggest desire to be like Jesus."

—LAURIE KOEHN, WNBA GUARD

"Follow God's example, therefore, as dearly loved children."

—EPHESIANS 5:1

Laurie Koehn scored 917 points during her career at Kansas State. She set the school mark for three-pointers in a game when she hit 10 in a game against Iowa.

AUGUST
5

"When we see that we are drifting spiritually, we know that God is right there for us— waiting to bring us back to Him."

—NATE MCLOUTH, MLB ALL-STAR OUTFIELDER

"We must pay the most careful attention, therefore, to what we have heard, so that we do not drift away."

—HEBREWS 2:1

After stealing 179 bases in 180 attempts in high school, Nate McLouth was drafted by the Pittsburgh Pirates. In 2013 he hit his 100th home run while playing for the Baltimore Orioles.

MAY 29

"Our love for our heavenly Father should be so powerful that there is no comparison between how much we love God and how much we love anyone else on earth."

—SHANNA ZOLMAN, WNBA GUARD

"Whoever does not carry their cross and follow me cannot be my disciple."

—LUKE 14:27

Shanna Zolman graduated from the University of Tennessee as the ninth highest scorer in Lady Vols basketball history with 1,706 points. She was drafted in 2006 by the WNBA San Antonio Silver Stars.

AUGUST 4

"My running is a gift from God. I would hope people would see that difference in me."

—ALLYSON FELIX,
OLYMPIC GOLD MEDAL–WINNING SPRINTER

"Walk by the Spirit, and you will not gratify the desires of the flesh."

—GALATIANS 5:16

Allyson Felix won her first Olympic gold medal in 2008 in Beijing in the 4 x 400-meter relay. In 2012 at London, she won her first individual Olympic gold by capturing the 200-meter race.

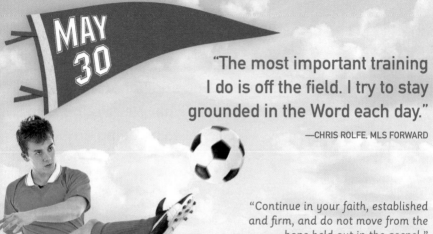

MAY 30

"The most important training I do is off the field. I try to stay grounded in the Word each day."

—CHRIS ROLFE, MLS FORWARD

"Continue in your faith, established and firm, and do not move from the hope held out in the gospel."

—COLOSSIANS 1:23

Chris Rolfe, who played collegiately at the University of Dayton and professionally for the Chicago Fire in the MLS, was inducted into the Ohio Soccer Hall of Fame in 2010.

AUGUST 3

"As long as we do our best for God's glory, we will be pleasing God and honoring Him—which is what we're supposed to be doing anyway."

—BETSY KING, LPGA HALL OF FAME GOLFER

"Do your best to present yourself to God as one approved, a worker who does not need to be ashamed and who correctly handles the word of truth."

—2 TIMOTHY 2:15

Betsy King is a member of the LPGA Hall of Fame. During her distinguished career, she won six majors and a total of 34 tournaments.

MAY 31

"No matter how much money we have, giving what we do have to help our brothers and sisters is what makes God smile on each of us."

—TAMIKA CATCHINGS, WNBA ALL-STAR FORWARD

"Love your neighbor as yourself."

—MATTHEW 22:39

Tamika Catchings didn't let a hearing disability stop her as a teenager. She persevered and became Ms. Basketball in Illinois as a high school player.

AUGUST 2

"We can be bold and courageous because God is with us—His Spirit is living inside us."

—RYAN HALL, OLYMPIC LONG-DISTANCE RUNNER

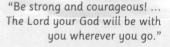

"Be strong and courageous! … The Lord your God will be with you wherever you go."

—JOSHUA 1:9

In 2008 Ryan Hall was named the Road Runner of the Year by Road Runners Club of America.

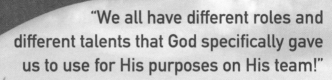

JUNE 1

"We all have different roles and different talents that God specifically gave us to use for His purposes on His team!"

—JENNY BOUCEK, WNBA PLAYER AND COACH

"Each of you should use whatever gift you have received to serve others, as faithful stewards of God's grace in its various forms."

—1 PETER 4:10

Jenny Boucek was the head coach of the WNBA's Sacramento Monarchs for three seasons.

AUGUST
1

"Put your focus on Christ. Put your focus on more important things in life."

—BEN ZOBRIST, MLB ALL-STAR SECOND BASEMAN

"Not that I have already obtained all this, or have already arrived at my goal, but I press on to take hold of that for which Christ Jesus took hold of me."

—PHILIPPIANS 3:12

Ben Zobrist's wife, Julianna, is a contemporary Christian music recording artist, and they both speak publicly about their faith.

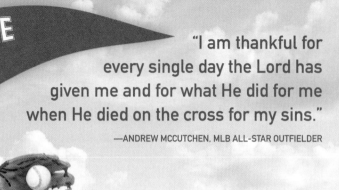

JUNE 2

"I am thankful for every single day the Lord has given me and for what He did for me when He died on the cross for my sins."

—ANDREW MCCUTCHEN, MLB ALL-STAR OUTFIELDER

"Thanks be to God for His indescribable gift!"

—2 CORINTHIANS 9:15

In 2013 Andrew McCutchen hit .317 with 21 home runs, 84 RBI, and 27 stolen bases to lead the Pirates to their first postseason action in 20 years.

JULY 31

"When we allow God to free us up, we live and play with more joy and peace."

—KIM BRAATZ-VOISARD, PROFESSIONAL BASEBALL PLAYER

"He has sent me to bind up the brokenhearted."

—ISAIAH 61:1

Playing for the only women's pro baseball team to play against men's pro teams in 1996, Kim hit the first female over-the-fence home run against a men's pro team.

JUNE 3

"Jesus needs to be given the praise that He deserves."

—GARY CARTER, MLB HALL OF FAME CATCHER

"Enter his gates with thanksgiving and his courts with praise; give thanks to him and praise his name."

—PSALM 100:4

In 2003 Gary Carter was selected to the Baseball Hall of Fame. He died of cancer in 2012 at the age of 57.

JULY 30

"Anyone can be nice to nice people. It takes a special person, one filled with the Holy Spirit, to love people who are not nice!"

—JENNY BOUCEK, WNBA PLAYER AND COACH

"As God's chosen people, holy and dearly loved, clothe yourselves with compassion, kindness, humility, gentleness and patience. Bear with each other and forgive one another if any of you has a grievance against someone."

—COLOSSIANS 3:12–13

While playing pro basketball in Iceland in 1998, Jenny Boucek was named the best player in the country.

JUNE 4

"We're all human.
We all make mistakes.
The only one who was perfect was
our Lord and Savior Jesus Christ."

—ALBERT PUJOLS, MLB ALL-STAR FIRST BASEMAN

"[Jesus] committed no sin and
no deceit was found in his mouth."

—1 PETER 2:22

A three-time Most Valuable Player in the National League with the
St. Louis Cardinals, Albert Pujols entered the 2014 season with a career batting
average of .321, second only to Joe Mauer among active players at the time.

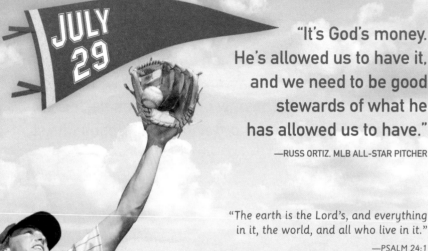

JULY 29

"It's God's money. He's allowed us to have it, and we need to be good stewards of what he has allowed us to have."

—RUSS ORTIZ. MLB ALL-STAR PITCHER

"The earth is the Lord's, and everything in it, the world, and all who live in it."

—PSALM 24:1

In 2003 Russ Ortiz made the National League All-Star team and led the league in wins with 21 victories while pitching for the Atlanta Braves.

JUNE 5

"Whatever God has made you to do, do it well for Him, for He is honored through excellence."

—SARA HALL, LONG-DISTANCE RUNNER

"In every matter of wisdom and understanding … the king found them [Daniel and friends] ten times better."

—DANIEL 1:20

Sara Hall's personal best in the 5,000 meter is 15:20:88.
For comparison's sake, that is the distance of a high school cross-country race.

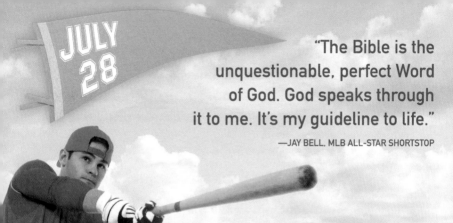

JULY 28

"The Bible is the unquestionable, perfect Word of God. God speaks through it to me. It's my guideline to life."

—JAY BELL, MLB ALL-STAR SHORTSTOP

"Your word is a lamp for my feet, a light on my path."

—PSALM 119:105

A first-round pick by the Minnesota Twins, Jay Bell played for Cleveland, Pittsburgh, Kansas City, Arizona, and the New York Mets during his career. He was an All-Star twice during his years in the big leagues. He became the Pirates' hitting coach in 2012.

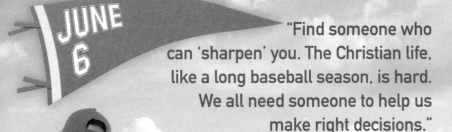

JUNE 6

"Find someone who can 'sharpen' you. The Christian life, like a long baseball season, is hard. We all need someone to help us make right decisions."

—RUSS ORTIZ,
MLB ALL-STAR PITCHER

"As iron sharpens iron, so one person sharpens another."

—PROVERBS 27:17

During his major league career from 1998 through 2010, Ortiz fashioned a career win-loss mark of 113–89 with 1,192 strikeouts.

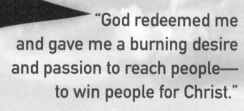

JULY 27

"God redeemed me and gave me a burning desire and passion to reach people— to win people for Christ."

—CHRISTIAN HOSOI, PROFESSIONAL SKATEBOARDER

"Therefore go and make disciples of all nations, baptizing them in the name of the Father and of the Son and of the Holy Spirit."

—MATTHEW 28:19

A multiple X-Games champion on his skateboard, Christian Hosoi began The Uprising, which uses skateboarding as a ministry.

JUNE 7

"I'm learning about God's plan, that His plan is a lot better than mine would have been."

—CASEY MARTIN, PGA GOLFER AND COLLEGE HEAD COACH

"Many are the plans in a person's heart, but it is the Lord's purpose that prevails."

—PROVERBS 19:21

Casey Martin, who was a teammate of Tiger Woods while at Stanford, became the golf coach at the University of Oregon in 2006.

JULY
26

"God alone is worthy of all the glory, honor, and praise."

—LAURIE KOEHN, WNBA GUARD

"Great is the Lord and most worthy of praise; his greatness no one can fathom."

—PSALM 145:3

To demonstrate her three-point-shooting prowess, Laurie Koehn once made 132 treys in 135 attempts in a five-minute time span.

JUNE 8

"The Lord does the most work in your life when you are in the desert."

—NICK HUNDLEY, MLB CATCHER

"See, I am doing a new thing! Now it springs up; do you not perceive it? I am making a way in the wilderness and streams in the wasteland."

—ISAIAH 43:19

In August of Nick Hundley's sixth season with the Padres, he and his wife, Amy, had their first child, a girl.

JULY 25

"Daily meditate on the Word of God and see how it changes your life."

—KEDRA HOLLAND-CORN, WNBA GUARD

"Keep this Book of the Law always on your lips; meditate on it day and night."

—JOSHUA 1:8

Kedra Holland-Corn spent seven years in the WNBA, scoring 1,938 points for Sacramento, Houston, and Detroit.

JUNE 9

"Seek God first and everything else will fall into place."

—RUTH RILEY, WNBA ALL-STAR CENTER

"Since, then, you have been raised with Christ, set your hearts on things above, where Christ is, seated at the right hand of God."

—COLOSSIANS 3:1

In her career, Ruth Riley has been both the Most Outstanding Player of the NCAA Women's Basketball Finals (2001) and the MVP of the WNBA Finals (2003).

JULY 24

"Depend on God's Word. That helps us trust His promises and His love."

—BEN CRANE, PGA GOLFER

"All Scripture is God-breathed and is useful for teaching."

—2 TIMOTHY 3:16

Ben and Heather Crane live in Texas, but he grew up in Oregon. It was there that his grandfather introduced him to golf when he was just five years old.

JUNE 10

"Try finding a verse you can memorize and keep in your heart so that during times of adversity, you can be encouraged and reminded to respond in a way that reflects Jesus."

—SIDNEY SPENCER, WNBA FORWARD

"They claim to know God but by their actions they deny him. They are detestable, disobedient and unfit for doing anything good."

—TITUS 1:16

While in college at the University of Tennessee, Sidney Spencer took time off from basketball to go on mission trips to Belize, Brazil, Costa Rica, and the Dominican Republic.

JULY 23

"We all need to be able to accept our failures like our victories, and vice versa. Live your life to the fullest with God's grace!"

—TAMIKA CATCHINGS, WNBA ALL-STAR FORWARD

"God resists the proud, but gives grace to the humble."

—JAMES 4:6
(NEW KING JAMES VERSION)

Tamika Catchings is one of two women's basketball players who accomplished a quintuple-double in a basketball game—both were high school girls. Catchings did it in 1997 when she had 25 points, 18 rebounds, 11 assists, 10 steals, and 10 blocked shots.

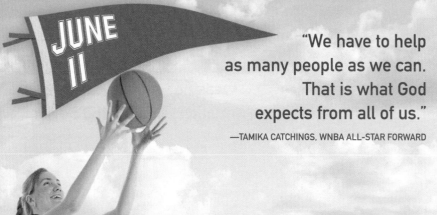

JUNE 11

"We have to help as many people as we can. That is what God expects from all of us."

—TAMIKA CATCHINGS, WNBA ALL-STAR FORWARD

"Do not forget to do good and to share with others, for with such sacrifices God is pleased."

—HEBREWS 13:16

Tamika Catchings, daughter of NBA player Harvey Catchings, has enjoyed an MVP (2011) career in the WNBA and three gold medal–winning appearances for the USA in the Olympics.

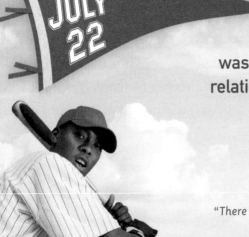

JULY 22

"Being a good guy was not enough. I needed a relationship with the Savior."

—WALT WEISS,
MLB ALL-STAR SHORTSTOP AND MANAGER

"There is no one righteous, not even one."

—ROMANS 3:10

Walt Weiss had a 14-year major league career during which he was the 1988 Rookie of the Year and a member of the 1998 NL All-Star team. He was coaching at his children's high school when the Colorado Rockies named him their manager heading into the 2013 season.

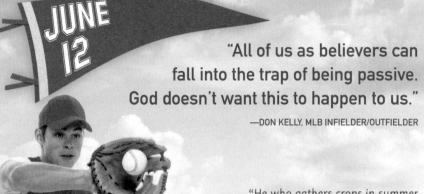

JUNE 12

"All of us as believers can fall into the trap of being passive. God doesn't want this to happen to us."

—DON KELLY, MLB INFIELDER/OUTFIELDER

"He who gathers crops in summer is a prudent son, but he who sleeps during harvest is a disgraceful son."

—PROVERBS 10:5

While playing for the Detroit Tigers, Don Kelly played every position, including a stint on the mound. As the 2014 season began, he was the only active player with that distinction.

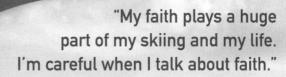

JULY 21

"My faith plays a huge part of my skiing and my life. I'm careful when I talk about faith."

—DAVID WISE, US OLYMPIC GOLD MEDAL–WINNING SNOWBOARDER

"I am sending you out as sheep among wolves. Therefore be as shrewd as snakes and as innocent as doves."

—MATTHEW 10:16

A multiple gold medal winner in the Winter X Games in the superpipe, David Wise captured gold at the 2014 Sochi Olympics in the halfpipe.

JUNE 13

"You can never out-give God."

—SIEW-AI LIM, LPGA GOLFER

"Bring the whole tithe into the storehouse."

—MALACHI 3:10

As a pro, Siew-Ai Lim enjoyed playing the guitar as a part of the LPGA Bible Fellowship that met while the golfers were on the Tour.

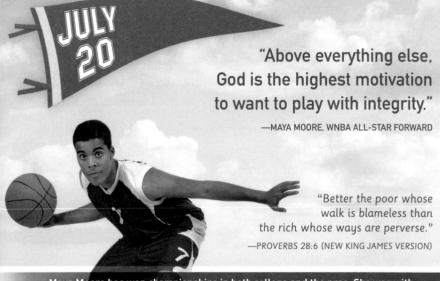

JULY 20

"Above everything else, God is the highest motivation to want to play with integrity."

—MAYA MOORE, WNBA ALL-STAR FORWARD

"Better the poor whose walk is blameless than the rich whose ways are perverse."

—PROVERBS 28:6 (NEW KING JAMES VERSION)

Maya Moore has won championships in both college and the pros. She was with Connecticut when the Lady Huskies won two national titles, and her Minnesota Lynx have also won multiple titles. She was WNBA Finals MVP in 2013.

"Being connected with Christ not only empowers us to take the step of faith to begin the journey but it also fuels our journey to ensure completion. Step out and hold on. See what God can do with you."

—KEDRA HOLLAND-CORN, WNBA GUARD

" 'Come,' [Jesus] said. Then Peter ... walked on the water."

—MATTHEW 14:29

Kedra Holland-Corn was named the Italian league's MVP during the 2005–2006 season while playing for La Spezia.

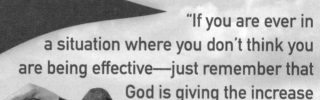

JULY 19

"If you are ever in a situation where you don't think you are being effective—just remember that God is giving the increase to your good works."

—JOHN REGISTER,
PARALYMPIC MEDAL WINNER

"For we are God's handiwork, created in Christ Jesus to do good works, which God prepared in advance for us to do."

—EPHESIANS 2:10

John Register was injured so severely while training to qualify as an Olympian in 1994 that his left leg had to be amputated. He went on to compete in the 1996 Paralympic Games.

JUNE 15

"If you can keep your eyes focused on the Lord and be faithful to Him and trust in Him, every day should be much easier to get through."

—RICK AGUILERA, MLB ALL-STAR PITCHER

"My eyes are ever on the Lord, for only he will release my feet from the snare."

—PSALM 25:15

After retiring as the Minnesota Twins' all-time saves leader (254), Rick Aguilera and his family moved to Santa Fe, California. Aguilera pitched in 732 games in his career, won 86 games, and saved 318.

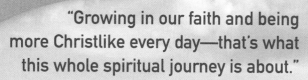

JULY 18

"Growing in our faith and being more Christlike every day—that's what this whole spiritual journey is about."

—TIM SALMON, MLB ALL-STAR OUTFIELDER

"Grow in the grace and knowledge of our Lord and Savior Jesus Christ. To him be glory both now and forever."

—2 PETER 3:18

From 1992 through 2006, Tim Salmon played for one team—the Angels. He was the AL Rookie of the Year in 1993. He hit 299 home runs and knocked in 1,016 runs for the Angels.

JUNE 16

"Let go of your struggles and let God be in control."

—SHANNA ZOLMAN, WNBA GUARD

"Whatever you have commanded us we will do, and wherever you send us we will go."

—JOSHUA 1:16

After her six-year WNBA career ended, Shanna Zolman joined the Fellowship of Christian Athletes, where she teaches clinics and works with college students to encourage them spiritually.

JULY 17

"Even though things may not always go as we had planned, in the end, if you keep your focus on Jesus, you will prosper."

—SIDNEY SPENCER, WNBA FORWARD

"For our light and momentary troubles are achieving for us an eternal glory that far outweighs them all. So we fix our eyes not on what is seen, but on what is unseen, since what is seen is temporary, but what is unseen is eternal."

—2 CORINTHIANS 4:17–18

Sidney Spencer's grandfather, Earl Spencer, played briefly for the New York Knickerbockers in the World War II era.

"Our Creator intentionally made us with a void in our heart. Sometimes we try to fill that with money, automobiles, drugs, or alcohol. The only thing that fills that void and [the only way to] experience eternal joy is your relationship with Jesus Christ."

—MIKE SWEENEY, MLB ALL-STAR FIRST BASEMAN

"Do not work for food that spoils, but for food that endures to eternal life, which the Son of Man will give you."

—JOHN 6:27

During his 15-year major league career, Mike Sweeney had a .297 batting average with 215 home runs and 909 RBIs. He made the All-Star team five times during his time with Kansas City.

"Have you accepted
God's free gift of forgiveness and
eternal life through His Son, Jesus Christ?"

—JOSH DAVIS,
OLYMPIC GOLD MEDAL–WINNING SWIMMER

"Jesus said ... , 'I am the resurrection and
the life. The one who believes in me will
live, even though they die; and whoever
lives by believing in me will never die.' "

—JOHN 11:25–26

Swimming for the United States, Josh Davis racked up five medals
in the Summer Olympic Games. In 1996 in Atlanta, Davis captured
three gold medals, and in Sydney in 2000, he won two silvers.

JUNE 18

"When I think of the men in the Bible I want to be like, it's David and Solomon—men who are wise."

—WEBB SIMPSON, PGA GOLFER

"Solomon's wisdom was greater than the wisdom of all the people of the East, and greater than all the wisdom of Egypt."

—1 KINGS 4:30

After playing golf at Wake Forest University and graduating in 2008, Webb Simpson joined the PGA Tour. He won a major in 2012—the US Open—as well as two other PGA tournaments through the end of the 2013 season.

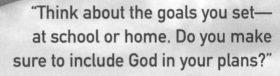

JULY 15

"Think about the goals you set—at school or home. Do you make sure to include God in your plans?"

—WENDY WARD, LPGA GOLFER

"In their hearts humans plan their course, but the Lord establishes their steps."

—PROVERBS 16:9

Four-time LPGA Tour event winner Wendy Ward and her husband, Nate, live on a ranch in Washington State.

JUNE 19

"Even when we walk through the valley, God is so faithful."

—BRANDON WEBB, MLB ALL-STAR PITCHER

"Even though I walk through the darkest valley, I will fear no evil, for you are with me."

—PSALM 23:4

Right-hander Brandon Webb won 10 games in his first season with the Arizona Diamondbacks. In a career shortened by injury, Webb went 87–62 with a 3.27 ERA.

"Take life one day at a time. God has promised this day alone. To live in the moment in the Lord is the most successful address to live at. We need to decide: 'Today I'm going to live for the Lord.'"

—NICK HUNDLEY, MLB CATCHER

"Therefore do not worry about tomorrow, for tomorrow will worry about itself. Each day has enough trouble of its own."

—MATTHEW 6:34

Catcher Nick Hundley had his best power numbers for San Diego in 2013 when he hit 13 home runs and knocked in 44 runs for the Padres.

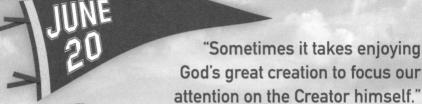

JUNE 20

"Sometimes it takes enjoying God's great creation to focus our attention on the Creator himself."

—DAVID FISHER, MLB CHAPLAIN

"Great are the works of the Lord; they are pondered by all who delight in them."

—PSALM 111:2

For nearly three decades, David Fisher served the Toronto Blue Jays as the team chaplain. His nephew is longtime NHL player Mike Fisher.

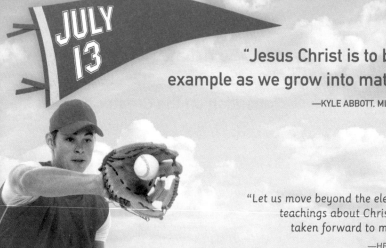

JULY 13

"Jesus Christ is to be our example as we grow into maturity."

—KYLE ABBOTT, MLB PITCHER

"Let us move beyond the elementary teachings about Christ and be taken forward to maturity."

—HEBREWS 6:1

Kyle Abbott played college baseball at Cal State Long Beach and UC San Diego before being drafted in 1989 by the California Angels. He pitched in the majors for four years.

"Remember, your trials—big or small—are the times when you can sense God's presence. 'Count it all joy when you fall into various trials' (James 1:2). Exercise your faith. God will never give you more weight than you can handle."

—ADRIAN WILLIAMS-STRONG, WNBA ALL-STAR FORWARD

"The apostles said to the Lord, 'Increase our faith!'"

—LUKE 17:5

During 2003, her best season in the WNBA, Adrian Williams averaged 10 points and 7 rebounds a game for the Phoenix Mercury.

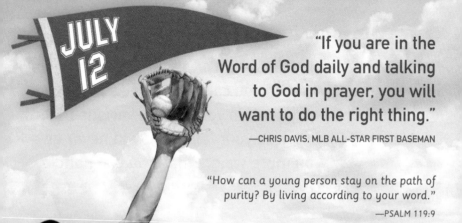

JULY 12

"If you are in the Word of God daily and talking to God in prayer, you will want to do the right thing."

—CHRIS DAVIS, MLB ALL-STAR FIRST BASEMAN

"How can a young person stay on the path of purity? By living according to your word."

—PSALM 119:9

"Pray continually."

—1 THESSALONIANS 5:17

Chris Davis had a breakout year in 2013, hitting 53 home runs (the 26th highest total in MLB history) and knocking in 138 runs for the Baltimore Orioles in his sixth year in the majors.

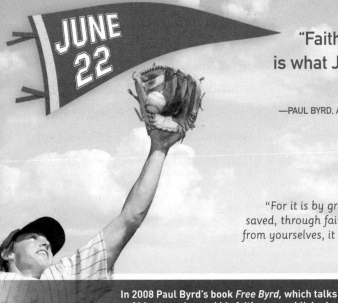

JUNE 22

"Faith, not works,
is what Jesus wants.
Trust Him."

—PAUL BYRD, ALL-STAR MLB PITCHER

"For it is by grace you have been
saved, through faith—and this is not
from yourselves, it is the gift of God."

—EPHESIANS 2:8

In 2008 Paul Byrd's book *Free Byrd*, which talks
of his struggles and his faith, was published.

"Baseball's a God-given talent. There are a lot of responsibilities that come with that. You need to find what you're passionate about off the field. I'm passionate about baseball and I love it. But off-the-field stuff means more."

—CLAYTON KERSHAW, MLB ALL-STAR PITCHER

"Each of you should give what you have decided in your heart to give, not reluctantly or under compulsion, for God loves a cheerful giver."

—2 CORINTHIANS 9:7

One of the best baseball pitchers of this era, Clayton Kershaw and his wife, Ellen, built Arise Home, an orphanage in Zambia.

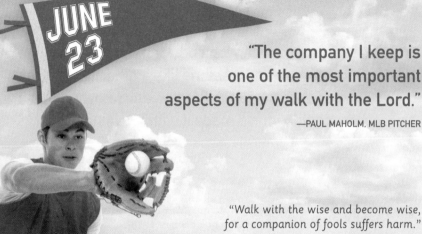

JUNE 23

"The company I keep is one of the most important aspects of my walk with the Lord."

—PAUL MAHOLM, MLB PITCHER

"Walk with the wise and become wise, for a companion of fools suffers harm."

—PROVERBS 13:20

Paul Maholm first pitched in the majors in 2005 for the Pittsburgh Pirates. Through the 2013 season, he had won 76 games as a starting pitcher. In February 2014 he signed a contract to pitch for the Los Angeles Dodgers.

JULY 10

"Success is a vapor. I can look back on my major league career, and it seems like a dream. What you recall are the tough times—and knowing that 'I couldn't have made it without Jesus Christ.'"

—TURNER WARD,
MLB OUTFIELDER

"Obey everything I have commanded you. And surely I am with you always, to the very end of the age."

—MATTHEW 28:20

In Turner Ward's best major league season as hitter, he batted .353 in 71 games for the Pittsburgh Pirates in 1997.

"When the day comes when I have to step away from baseball, I hope people say I made an impact for the Lord by playing the game with passion and that I was a bold witness for Him."

—CHASE HEADLEY, MLB THIRD BASEMAN

"Since we have such a hope, we are very bold."

—2 CORINTHIANS 3:12

The San Diego Padres drafted Chase Headley in 2005, and he first played for the team at the major league level in 2007. In 2012 he hit 31 home runs and knocked in 115 runs for San Diego.

JULY

9

"The beauty of putting your heart into the Lord's hands is that He will do amazing things with your life."

—MARIANO RIVERA, MLB ALL-STAR PITCHER

"This is what the Lord says, ... 'Call to me and I will answer you and tell you great and unsearchable things you do not know.' "

—JEREMIAH 33:2–3

Mariano Rivera was the only player ever to be named the MVP of the World Series, a league championship series, and the All-Star Game.

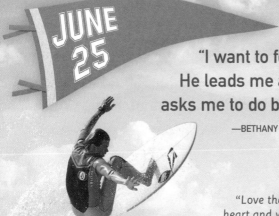

JUNE 25

"I want to follow God wherever He leads me and do whatever He asks me to do because I trust Him."

—BETHANY HAMILTON DIRKS, CHAMPION SURFER

"Love the Lord your God with all your heart and with all your soul and with all your strength and with all your mind."

—LUKE 10:27

In 2004 Bethany Hamilton received the ESPY Award for Best Comeback Athlete.

"I want to perform well for my teammates and the fans, but I'm playing for the honor and glory of Jesus Christ."

—JAKE PEAVY, MLB ALL-STAR PITCHER

"So whether you eat or drink or whatever you do, do it all for the glory of God."

—1 CORINTHIANS 10:31

Jake Peavy's major league career began in 2002 with the San Diego Padres. Over the next 12 years, he won 132 games and the 2007 National League Cy Young Award.

JUNE 26

"We need to listen to the Holy Spirit, ask Him for help, and then be obedient to Him."

—AARON BADDELEY, PGA GOLFER

"But when he, the Spirit of truth, comes, he will guide you into all the truth."

—JOHN 16:13

On the PGA Tour, Aaron Baddeley has won the 2006 Verizon Heritage, the 2007 FBR Open, and the 2011 Northern Trust Open. He and his wife, Richelle, live in Scottsdale, Arizona.

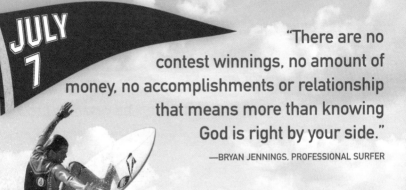

JULY 7

"There are no contest winnings, no amount of money, no accomplishments or relationship that means more than knowing God is right by your side."

—BRYAN JENNINGS, PROFESSIONAL SURFER

"We know and rely on the love God has for us. God is love. Whoever lives in love lives in God, and God in them."

—1 JOHN 4:16

Bryan Jennings was a professional surfer by the time he was 18 years old. In 1995 he founded Walking on Water, a ministry that reaches out to young people who love surfing.

JUNE 27

"When we are in the middle of tough times, we need to believe God's Word and not our negative thoughts."

—BEN CRANE, PGA GOLFER

"[God] is able to do immeasurably more than all we ask or imagine."

—EPHESIANS 3:20

Ben Crane won PGA tournaments in 2003 (Bell Classic), 2005 (US Bank Championship), 2010 (Farmers Insurance Open), and 2011 (McGladrey Classic).

"We are not designed to walk on this earth alone—even Jesus had 12 disciples who were his support system. Are you and your friends helping each other be better Christians?"

—BRYAN CLAY, OLYMPIC GOLD MEDAL–WINNING DECATHLETE

"A friend loves at all times, and a brother is born for a time of adversity."

—PROVERBS 17:17

Bryan Clay won the gold medal in the decathlon in the 2008 Olympic Games in Beijing after capturing silver in Athens in 2004.

JUNE 28

"God is with me in
the good times and the bad."

—MICHAEL BARRETT, MLB CATCHER

"Offer your bodies as a living sacrifice,
holy and pleasing to God."

—ROMANS 12:1

After beginning his major league career with the Montreal Expos, Michael Barrett
played at Wrigley Field for over three seasons with the Chicago Cubs.
His cousin Scott Fletcher had also played for the Cubs.

JULY 5

"We never shine brighter than when we are reflecting God's glory."

—KIM BRAATZ-VOISARD, PROFESSIONAL BASEBALL PLAYER

"And we all, who with unveiled faces contemplate the Lord's glory, are being transformed into his image with ever-increasing glory, which comes from the Lord, who is the Spirit."

—2 CORINTHIANS 3:18

From 1994 through 1997 Kim played for the Colorado Silver Bullets, an American women's pro baseball team. Among her highlights was hitting a home run against a men's team in 1996.

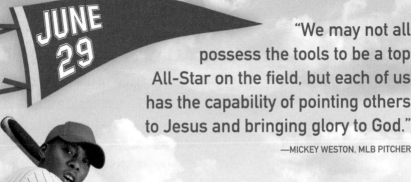

JUNE 29

"We may not all possess the tools to be a top All-Star on the field, but each of us has the capability of pointing others to Jesus and bringing glory to God."

—MICKEY WESTON, MLB PITCHER

"So do not be ashamed of the testimony about our Lord."

—2 TIMOTHY 1:8

Flint, Michigan's Mickey Weston pitched in parts of five major league seasons before retiring in 1993. Weston works with Unlimited Potential, Inc. (UPI), a ministry to major leaguer players.

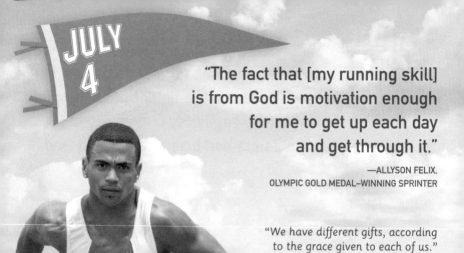

JULY
4

"The fact that [my running skill] is from God is motivation enough for me to get up each day and get through it."

—ALLYSON FELIX,
OLYMPIC GOLD MEDAL–WINNING SPRINTER

"We have different gifts, according to the grace given to each of us."

—ROMANS 12:6

Allyson Felix was the first woman to win three world titles in the 200-meter race when she captured the 200-meter at the 2009 IAAF World Outdoor Championships.

JUNE 30

"It's time for us Christians to get in the batter's box—to make sure our belief results in action."

—MATT DIAZ, MLB OUTFIELDER

"For God so loved the world that he gave his one and only Son."

—JOHN 3:16

Matt Diaz grew up in Lakeland, Florida, where his dad, Ed, was the spring training chaplain for the Detroit Tigers. His mom, Gwen, is a successful freelance writer and public speaker. Diaz retired in 2013 with a career batting average of .290.

JULY 3

"Even if no one else is there for me, Jesus always is."

—ZINA GARRISON,
GRAND SLAM TENNIS CHAMPION

"Never will I leave you;
never will I forsake you."

—HEBREWS 13:5

During a professional tennis career in the 1980s and 1990s, Zina Garrison won 14 titles and had a record of 587–270. She won the Australian Open (once) and Wimbledon (twice) in mixed doubles.

JULY 1

"Trials are opportunities [for God] to work through us in the middle of challenging situations."

—MIKE MAROTH, MLB PITCHER

"Be joyful in hope, patient in affliction, faithful in prayer."

—ROMANS 12:12

Mike Maroth won 14 games for the Detroit Tigers in 2005.

JULY 2

"I seek to demonstrate what God has done for me and that He can do it in others' lives as well."

—KAKÀ, BRAZILIAN SOCCER MIDFIELDER

"You are the light of the world. A town built on a hill cannot be hidden. Neither do people light a lamp and put it under a bowl. Instead they put it on its stand, and it gives light to everyone in the house. In the same way, let your light shine before others, that they may see your good deeds and glorify your Father in heaven."

—MATTHEW 5:14–16

In 2007 Kaká, who was born in Brasilia, Brazil, was named the European Footballer of the Year and FIFA World Player of the Year. He spent that year playing for Milan.